Tibetan Mastiff Puppies & Dogs

Step by Step Book… care, health, diet, training, behavior and more…

By Susan Shaw

Copyright and Trademarks

All rights reserved. No part of this book may be reproduced or transferred in any form or by any means without the written permission of the publisher and author. This publication is Copyright 2014 by World Ideas Ltd / BLEP Publishing. All products, publications, software and services mentioned in this publication are protected by trademarks.

Disclaimer and Legal Notice

This product is not legal, accounting, medical or health advice and should not be interpreted in that manner. You need to do your own due-diligence to determine if the content of this product is right for you and your animals. While we have tried to verify the information in this publication, neither the author, publisher nor the affiliates assume any responsibility for errors, omissions or contrary interpretation of the subject matter herein.

We have no control over the nature, content and availability of the websites, products or sources listed in this book. The inclusion of any website links does not necessarily imply a recommendation or endorsement of the views expressed within them. We may receive payment if you order a product or service using a link contained within this book. BLEP Publishing or the author take no responsibility or will not be liable for the websites or content being unavailable or removed.

The advice and strategies, contained herein may not be suitable for every individual or animal / pet. The author and publisher shall not be liable for any loss incurred as a consequence of the use and or the application, directly or indirectly, of any information presented in this work. This publication is designed to provide information in regard to the subject matter covered.

Neither the author nor the publisher assume any responsibility for any errors or omissions, nor do they represent or warrant that the information, ideas, plans, actions, suggestions, and methods of operation contained herein is in all cases true, accurate, appropriate, or legal. It is the reader's responsibility to consult with his or her own advisor before putting any of the enclosed information, ideas, or practices written in this book into practice.

Foreword

There are many legends associated with the origins of the Tibetan Mastiff. One suggests that in a great period of ice and snow, a god descended from the heavens to save the Tibetan people. He came astride a massive dog that was the forerunner of the Tibetan Mastiff.

Other stories suggest that the dogs are the descendants of a species of lion now extinct in the Himalayas, or that they are the offspring of a mating between dogs and black bears.

It is claimed that among his troops, the Mongol chieftain Genghis Khan had 50,000 Tibetan Mastiff "soldiers." The dogs were said to feed on the bodies of their dead enemies and to perform battlefield exploits deeply satisfying to the ruthless Khan.

Historians don't dispute that Tibetan Mastiffs went to war with the Great Khan, but it is doubtful that more than a dozen or so of the dogs accompanied his troops. The dogs' fierceness is also not in dispute, and was first chronicled by Marco Polo who encountered the breed serving in one of their traditional roles, acting as guardians for trading caravans.

In the modern canine world, the Tibetan Mastiff, though classed as a working dog for show purposes, is still a relatively rare breed. More importantly, however, these dogs originated under rarefied circumstances in the high ranges of the Himalayas.

Foreword

There, Tibetan Mastiffs were revered as guardians for households and flocks, as well as serving as temple dogs. It is believed the Buddha owned one of the great dogs, and those with white stars on their chests are thought to possess unusually brave hearts.

It's easy to understand why mystical significance would be attached to these massive and majestic dogs with their pluming and curved tails, deep plush coats, and voices like temple gongs.

Deeply devoted to their masters, and suspicious to the point of viciousness with strangers, many will play with kittens and puppies with utter tenderness. They are not guard dogs per se after the fashion of a German Shepherd or a Rottweiler. They are guardians, driving perceived threats away with physical and vocal intimidation.

Make no mistake. This is not a breed for everyone or for a casual dog owner. The Tibetan Mastiff bonds deeply with its owner and requires proper training to channel its instinctual protective urges.

These dogs have an unusual capacity for independent thought. Traditionally they were allowed to roam by night to perform their duties, which necessitated forming the capacity to make decisions and choices on their own.

The consequences of allowing a Tibetan Mastiff to be bored is akin to a force of mass destruction. They can and will destroy anything, and may act out aggressively against inanimate objects just to channel their thwarted urge to do their job. For no reason whatsoever, your dog may decide a lawn chair is "the enemy" and completely demolish it.

Although quite capable of being a good family dog, the Tibetan Mastiff is not a pet to be adopted on a whim without proper education on the eccentricities of the breed. It is also possible that the average person might not be able to afford the purchase or even to locate a dog to buy.

An average "street" price from a reputable kennel will be around $3000 / £1748, but in 2011 an 11-month-old rare, red Tibetan Mastiff named Big Splash sold for $1.5 million (£874,452), gaining for himself the title of "most expensive dog in the world." The dog's services as a stud were subsequently sold for $100,000 / £58,296 an "engagement."

China Tibet Online relates the following story under the headline, "One Dog Beating Five Wolves:"

"On a winter night in 1992, at the 4,000-meter high altitude township of Awancang, Maqu County in Gannan Tibetan Autonomous Prefecture, Gansu Province, the Tibetan Mastiff named 'Gold Panther' was sleeping beside his master's tent.

Suddenly, he found five hungry wolves breaking in the sheepfold. When his master arrived, Gold Panther had been wounded and his body was bleeding all over. Beside him, there were the dead bodies of the five wolves."

There is, without question, something epic and intriguing about a breed brave enough and dedicated enough to take on five wolves. The Tibetan Mastiff's reputation is hard earned and well deserved. There truly is no breed quite like the Great Dog of Tibet.

Foreword

Contents

Foreword 1
Chapter 1 – Introduction to The Tibetan Mastiff 10
   Similar Breeds 14
      Bangara Mastiff 14
      Bhotia (Himalayan Sheepdog) 15
      Kyi Apso 15
Chapter 2 – Buying a Tibetan Mastiff 17
   The Most Expensive Dog in the World 18
   Geography Does Not Dictate Kennel Choice 19
   Cost as a Deciding Factor 19
   The Obvious Questions 20
   Sometimes Breeders Say No 24
   Additional Relative Information 25
   Materials the Breeder Should Provide 26
   Identification Systems Used 27
   Are You Working With a Bad Breeder? 28
Chapter 3 – Is This The Right Dog For Me? 31
   The Tibetan Mastiff 32
      Instinct to Protect 32
      Independent Decision Maker 33
      Training Considerations 34

Physical Characteristics 36
    Types of Tibetan Mastiff 36
    Body Conformation and Size 37
    Coat and Colors 37
    Health Considerations 38
Serious Pre-Adoption Considerations 39
Chapter 4 – Caring for Your Tibetan Mastiff 43
Managing Your Dog's Diet 43
    Selecting Food for Your Dog 44
Nutritional Transitions 45
    A Puppy's Diet 46
    An Adult Diet 46
    A Senior Diet 47
Feeding Schedules 48
The Danger of Bloat 48
Specific Dietary Cautions 49
Avoid Popular Rawhide Chews 52
The Importance of Clean Water 53
Exercising Your Tibetan Mastiff 53
Coat Maintenance and Grooming 54
    Grooming as Preventive "Medicine" 56
Bathing Your Dog 56

Foreword

Cleaning Your Dog's Ears 58

Eye Care 58

Dental Care 59

Nail Clipping or Grinding? 61

Anal Gland Maintenance 62

Traveling with a Tibetan Mastiff 63

Boarding 66

Chapter 5 – Training Your Tibetan Mastiff 67

The Critical First Year 67

    Crating and Containing Puppies 69

The Difficulties of Adult Adoptions 71

Dogs Respond Well to Routine 72

Housebreaking: The First Important Routine 73

Collars / Harnesses and Leads 75

Basic Training Exercises 75

    Sit 76

    Down 77

    Stay 78

Come 78

    Heel 79

Cutting Back on the Treats as Rewards 80

Attending Classes or Obtaining a Trainer 81

Chapter 6 – Tibetan Mastiff Health 83
   Adopting a Healthy Dog 83
   Early Medical Care 84
   Dental Health 85
   Finding A Good Veterinarian 86
   Annual Vet Visits 88
   Vaccinations 89
      Rabies 89
      Parvovirus 89
      Distemper 90
      Kennel Cough 90
      Lyme Disease 91
   The Debate Over Vaccinations 91
   Spaying and Neutering 92
   Fleas 93
   Ticks 96
   Mosquito Control and Heartworms 97
   Internal Parasites 98
   Hot Spots 99
   Entropion and Ectropion 100
   Hip and Elbow Dysplasia 101
   Canine Inherited Demyelinative Neuropathy 102

Foreword

Hypertrophic Cardiomyopathy	102
The Cost of Veterinary Care	103
Chapter 7 – Showing Tibetan Mastiffs	**106**
Dog Show Basics	107
The Judges	108
Some Dog Show Terminology	109
Join a Breed Club	112
Chapter 8 – Tibetan Mastiff Breeders	**113**
United States	113
United Kingdom	114
Afterword	116
Appendix 1 - Breed Standard – United States	119
Relevant Websites	127
Glossary	129
Index	138

Chapter 1 – Introduction to The Tibetan Mastiff

Although not as generally well known as other breeds, the Tibetan Mastiff has contributed to the evolution of many familiar livestock-guardian dogs including the Bernese Mountain Dog, St. Bernard, Newfoundland, Komondor, Neapolitan Mastiff, Dogue de Bordeaux and Mastiff.

The Tibetan Mastiff, named for the land of his origin, is a natural purebred dog whose history perhaps extends backwards to 3000 BC. Early rock carvings depict dogs

Chapter 1 – Introduction to The Tibetan Mastiff

clearly of the mastiff type in the company of people. This evidence has fueled speculation that the Tibetan Mastiff may be the oldest of all the large breeds.

Marco Polo's account of his 1271 journey to the Orient includes the first documented evidence of the existence of the Tibetan Mastiff, which the explorer encountered in the Szechuan province of China. The dogs, described in the account as being "the size of donkeys," traveled with Tibetan traders as protection against tigers.

One of the dogs is believed to have also accompanied Marco Polo on his journeys and went with him at least part of the way on his return to Europe. There is, however, no record of the animal surviving to reach Italy.

The description of dogs as large as beasts of burden has to be taken with a grain of salt. Donkeys native to the region are much smaller than those we have in the West. Still, there are credible modern reports of dogs living in Tibet that are significantly larger than the breed standard requirements published by the English Kennel Club.

Individual specimens in Tibet have been recorded as standing 36 inches (91.5 cm) high at the shoulder. That's 10 inches (25.5 cm) greater than the minimum required height in the breed standard!

In the high table land of Tibet where the altitude varies from 10,500-16,400 feet (3,200-5,000 meters), these massive dogs evolved to cope with the demands of a barren landscape. Temperature extremes fluctuate from 3 F to 100

Chapter 1 – Introduction to The Tibetan Mastiff

F (-16-37.7 C) and can rise from below freezing cold to scorching heat in a single day.

(The average annual rainfall in Tibet ranges from 4-12 inches / 100-300 millimeters, so while the dogs can take almost any level of cold, they do not do well with damp, wet conditions.)

Traditionally, Tibetan Mastiffs guarded land and property including pastoral flocks, whole villages, trading caravans, and monasteries. As livestock guardians, they were well equipped to drive marauding wolves and leopards away from yaks, goats, and sheep.

In 1774 George Bogle, traveling in Tibet as part of a mission to establish trade relations, described the dogs he saw as extremely fierce and "shagged like a lion."

He reported that the animals were kept chained during the day, but set loose at night to patrol for predators and human intruders. Later accounts characterized the dogs as too vicious to approach unless their masters were with them.

In 1847 Lord Hardinge, the Viceroy of India, gifted Queen Victoria with a Tibetan Mastiff, and the future Edward VII owned one in 1874. That dog was widely exhibited, thus drawing attention to the breed.

Some accounts from this period are muddled, however, as Tibetan Mastiffs are not the only large dogs indigenous to the Himalayas.

Chapter 1 – Introduction to The Tibetan Mastiff

Colonel and Mrs. Eric Bailey brought a number of Tibetan Mastiffs to England in the early 20th century. In the 1930s, they helped to clarify the breed standard of several Tibetan dogs, including the Tibetan Mastiff.

The dogs did not reach the United States until 1958 when a pair was given to President Dwight D. Eisenhower who passed them on to Senator Harry Darby.

The foundation dog in the U.S., however, was Jumla's Kalu of Jumla, owned by Ann Rohrer of the Langtang kennel in Pearblossom, California. He was the first stud registered with The Tibetan Mastiff Club (which became the American Tibetan Mastiff Association.)

Part of the impetus for bringing the dogs to the U.S. was the realization that they faced extinction in their native land following the Chinese occupation of Tibet in 1959.

The Communists insisted the dogs be destroyed or their owners faced death themselves. Those animals that survived this tyrannical edict were bred in secret and taken out of Tibet by people dedicated to preserving this ancient breed. Had it not been for their efforts, a truly noble line of dogs would have passed into oblivion.

In the United States, the Tibetan Mastiff Club (TTMC) was incorporated in 1974 and its registry and studbook established the following year.

The Tibetan Mastiff competed as a rare breed until the American Kennel Club accepted it as a recognized working breed in January 2007. In the UK the Kennel Club also classifies the Tibetan Mastiff as a recognized working breed.

Similar Breeds

Although none of the other large breeds from the region are identical to the Tibetan Mastiff, all have, at one time or another been confused with these unique animals.

In part this is due to the fact that all of the breeds have at some point served as livestock or property guardians. Others, however, have also been used for hunting and, regrettably, dog fighting.

Bangara Mastiff

There is some tendency to confuse the Bangara Mastiff with another large dog from the region, the Bhotia. The modern Bangara breed was cultivated from the Tibetan Mastiff specifically to serve as a guardian for yak herds.

The Bangara also should not be mistaken for the Banjara (Ban-Djara) Mastiff or the Banjara Hound. The Bangara is a large, powerful, and very stubborn breed that displays marked aggression toward other dogs and has even been used in staged fighting competitions.

It has a square body with a deep chest and broad shoulders. The black and tan coat is long and harsh, with some white markings on the chest and feet. The dogs average 27 inches / 0.68 meters in height.

Bhotia (Himalayan Sheepdog)

The Himalayan Sheepdog is a livestock guardian indigenous to Nepal. It is a mountain dog closely related to both the Tibetan Mastiff and various Indian mastiffs.

The breed enjoys life in the outdoors and is rarely seen outside India and Nepal. It is both powerful and robust, and is regionally popular as a companion species.

The dogs are black and tan or apricot. Males typically stand 23-25 inches / 0.58-0.63 meters with females at 20-23 inches / 0.5-0.58 meters.

Kyi Apso

The Kyi Apso is a large livestock guardian breed used by the nomadic peoples of Tibet to protect sheep, goats, and yaks. In off duty hours this is a laidback, mellow breed.

Like the Tibetan Mastiff, the Kyi Apso is a large dog, standing approximately 28 inches / 0.71 meters and weighing in at around 100 lbs. / 45.35 kg. Their coats are 3-6 inches in length / 7.62-15.24 cm.

Any coat color is permitted and the breed is highly athletic with almost no tendency to become overweight.

Shakhi (Tibetan Hunting Dog)

The Shakhi or Tibetan Hunting Dog is extremely rare in comparison to other breeds from Tibet, Nepal, and the rest

Chapter 1 – Introduction to The Tibetan Mastiff

of Central Asia. It is also a guardian species, a herding animal, and a superb hunter.

There are two traditional types of Shakhi, delineated by size and color. Those used for hunting are generally white with red, black or brown markings. The dogs have a light frame, but are muscular and strong. The breed has a spitz tail with a dense, rough coat that is weatherproof. The average height is approximately 22 inches / 0.56 meters.

Chapter 2 – Buying a Tibetan Mastiff

The first step in buying a Tibetan Mastiff is finding a reputable breeder. Regardless of the venue through which you initially contact a breeder, be prepared to engage in a two-way exchange of information.

The breeder will want to screen you as a prospective buyer and you will want to find out the quality of the kennel and its bloodlines.

Legitimate breeders welcome inquiries about their breeding programs and schedule for upcoming litters, and legitimate

Chapter 2 – Buying a Tibetan Mastiff

buyers should have no issue with proving themselves to be appropriate prospective "parents."

The Most Expensive Dog in the World

If you have gone online and searched for prices on the Tibetan Mastiff, which I'm sure you have, you will discover that some individuals have sold for millions of dollars. These animals are incredibly rare, and especially fine specimens are, indeed, some of the most expensive dogs in the world.

Millionaire enthusiasts will have no difficulty paying that price to own an exceptional and rare animal, but you may be sweating bullets at the thought. It is actually very difficult to get exact price quotes for a Tibetan Mastiff. Most kennels will indicate on their websites that you have to call to discuss price. That's fine. It's worth the phone call to know exactly what you're dealing with.

Because the breed is growing rapidly in popularity in the United States and the United Kingdom, it is possible to find pet quality puppies for around $3000 / £1748. You may have to make a lot of those phone calls, but if you are absolutely determined to own a Tibetan Mastiff, you can.

A Malaysian millionaire, Kenny Lai, bought nine Tibetan Mastiffs in 2008 for £3.2 million (about $5.5 million USD). His dogs, now 30 in number, have the run of a 5000 square meter compound complete with air conditioning. The animals are worth more than £8 million (more than $13 million USD.)

Chapter 2 – Buying a Tibetan Mastiff

Geography Does Not Dictate Kennel Choice

Working within the constraints of geography might make sense for some breeds, but Tibetan Mastiffs are still relatively rare. If there is a breeder in your locale, you should certainly visit their establishment, but proximity is not a guarantee of a good working match in negotiating a purchase.

Dealing with a breeder at a distance is not the same thing as "buying a dog over the Internet," which implies a sight unseen and potentially shady deal. Thanks to technological advances in video communication, it is clearly possible to see puppies available for adoption in real time, to "meet" their parents, and to "tour" the kennel.

Granted, a breeder walking you through his operation on an iPad is not the same as being there and taking in all the details of the kennel on your own, but it is still a viable means of conducting a transaction.

I am not personally a fan of shipping live animals, so a purchase made at a distance should, in my opinion, conclude with a trip to retrieve the animal and bring it home. This added expense will have to be factored in to the overall cost of adopting the dog, and will vary greatly by circumstance.

Cost as a Deciding Factor

Clearly cost is a deciding factor and may prohibit the average buyer from acquiring a Tibetan Mastiff puppy.

Chapter 2 – Buying a Tibetan Mastiff

While it may seem crass to characterize the adoption of a live animal in terms of "return on investment," Tibetan Mastiffs are unusually long-lived for a large dog and can easily be with you for 10-14 years.

This is music to a prospective dog owner's ears, but also should give you pause to consider the expense of your purchase in both the short and long term. Surprisingly, Tibetan Mastiffs eat little in relation to their size, thriving on 4-5 cups of high-quality dry dog food per day. Over their lifetime, they are actually less expensive to feed than other large dog breeds.

Facts such as these can offset reluctance over the initial purchase price and any associated travel costs. Purchase price is typically determined by the puppy's status as "pet" or "show" quality. "Pet" quality puppies are judged to deviate sufficiently from the accepted breed standard to be inappropriate for use in a breeding program. They are thus offered at lower rates to prospective buyers.

"Show" quality animals are more expensive. Some breeders, however, offer all their puppies at one fixed rate. These are facts about which you need to be clear from the beginning of your purchase negotiations.

The Obvious Questions

If you've never adopted a pedigreed dog, especially a rare one, the "obvious" questions might not be obvious to you at all. To that end, I suggest you inquire about all the following points:

Chapter 2 – Buying a Tibetan Mastiff

- How long has the kennel been in operation and how long has the breeder worked with Tibetan Mastiffs?

- What is the primary goal of their breeding program? What is the overall health, temperament, and conformation of their dogs in general?

- Are other dogs raised at the facility? If so, what breeds and why? (Be cautious about kennels that house multiple breeds and seem to have a constant supply of puppies. They could be puppy "mills.")

- How many dogs are housed at the kennel and how many litters are produced annually?

- At what age are females allowed to have their first litter? (The answer should be after age 2.)

- How many litters are females allowed to have in their lifetime? (This should be no more than 3 or 4.)

- Why medical care is provided for pregnant and nursing mothers?

- Can you see the health records for the breeding pair?

- What are the strengths and weaknesses of Tibetan Mastiffs in terms of overall health? (This is a topic I will discuss more fully later in this book.)

- With what professional/breed based organizations are the breeder's dogs registered? Can you see proof

Chapter 2 – Buying a Tibetan Mastiff

of these registrations / memberships? What standards are required for dogs and their owners to qualify for membership in these groups?

- How far back does the breeder's line go and can you see photos of multiple generations of their dogs with explanations of their relationships?

- How are puppies socialized prior to adoption?

- Have the puppies received their first vaccinations and how does the breeder feel about some of the controversies associated with vaccinations and injection-site tumors?

- Have the puppies required any other kind of health care? If so, what and why?

- Are puppies marked with individual tattoos are microchips?

- Will you be allowed to select your puppy or will one be selected for you?

- If air travel is being considered as a means to deliver the puppy how will this be handled, what precautions will be taken, and how experienced is the breeder in the process?

- How old will the puppy have to be before you can take it home? (The correct answer is 8-12 weeks. Younger dogs are not ready to be separated from

Chapter 2 – Buying a Tibetan Mastiff

their mothers and litter mates, nor have they had a chance to be properly socialized.)

- Should it become necessary for you to surrender the dog at some future time, will the breeder take the animal back? If so, under what conditions?

- If, for whatever reason, you don't think working with this breeder is a good fit, do they network with other breeders and can they recommend other kennels?

(You want an affirmative answer to that last point. Any breeder should realize distance could be a deal breaker, and should be so passionate about the breed they do not see other breeders as competitors, but rather as colleagues.)

As you receive answers to these questions, get a sense of the breeder's demeanor. Are they forthcoming? Do they talk about positives and negatives of the breed? Do they ask as many questions as they answer?

A good breeder will want to know about you and your family, your lifestyle, and your home. They should clearly care about the welfare of the puppy in the long term. The exchange should, however, be cordial, pleasant, and enjoyable.

The kennel should provide you with a comprehensive packet of information on the Tibetan Mastiff breed, and on the puppy you are considering purchasing. All sales should center on a signed contract with clearly defined terms.

Chapter 2 – Buying a Tibetan Mastiff

The breeder should be prepared to discuss each of these terms, including specific health and money-back guarantees. If you feel rushed or pressured to "seal the deal," something is wrong. Also, if you ask questions that are deflected away from the topic, be suspicious.

Sometimes Breeders Say No

You should be prepared for the fact that the breeder may say no to the deal. Remember, the adoption process should be a two-way exchange of information. Make no mistake. You are being evaluated.

A breeder who is completely dedicated to the welfare of his dogs is willing to turn away a prospective client if they do not believe the puppy would be going to an appropriate home. To high-quality breeders, raising dogs is not so much a business as a calling and a passion.

With a breed as rare and as behaviorally specific as the Tibetan Mastiff, you should listen to any concerns a breeder expresses about your qualifications as a "parent." If more than one breeder declines your efforts to adopt a dog and cites similar reasons for their refusal, this should be a serious red flag.

A refusal may be based on something as simple and practical as the fact that your home is not structurally or spatially correct for a breed as large as the Tibetan Mastiff. Wonderful as these dogs may be, they are not appropriate pets for all households and they certainly are not a good "first time" dog.

Chapter 2 – Buying a Tibetan Mastiff

Additional Relative Information

As you evaluate the total terms of the adoption, there are other bits of information you will need to obtain from the breeder:

- Will the breeder be a resource to you throughout your dog's life, sharing their knowledge of the breed to help you make good choices for your dog as it matures?

- Will the breeder assist you with all official documentation and registration and are there any requirements that must be met before you will take possession of the dog's papers?

Chapter 2 – Buying a Tibetan Mastiff

- If you become so enamored of the breed that you want to begin raising Tibetan Mastiffs yourself, will your breeder help you to make connections and get started?*

*Be cautious of adoptions that actually require you to agree to allow the animal to participate in a breeding program unless you are prepared to make that commitment.

Breeders whose prices are slightly higher, but who are willing to help you learn about and care for your dog are offering you a higher return on your purchase investment.

Materials the Breeder Should Provide

If the adoption does indeed proceed, you should receive all of the following, and the breeder should be prepared to discuss details of each and address your questions.

- A contract explaining the responsibility of both parties in the adoption and the procedure whereby the puppy's papers are transferred into your name.

- Written information concerning such matters as diet, training / exercise, and routine healthcare including vaccinations and worming.

- A handwritten or official copy of the dog's pedigree (ancestry).

- Copies of all health records pertaining to the puppy including a schedule of booster shots required. Good breeders also disclose all potential genetic health conditions and discuss any screenings that have been performed. (I'll discuss this more fully in a later chapter.)

Typically the contract will also contain a guarantee of health at the time of adoption with a stipulation that a veterinarian verifies the fact within a set period of time.

You will likely be asked to provide written proof that this examination has occurred so that the health guarantees of the contract will remain in force.

Identification Systems Used

Most pedigreed dogs will be permanently identified in some way, usually with either a tattoo or an implanted microchip. Systems vary with each governing organization. The American Kennel Club, for instance, recommends permanent identification as a "common sense" practice.

The Kennel Club in the UK is accredited by the United Kingdom Accreditation Service and certifies dog breeders through the Kennel Club Assured Breeder Scheme. Member breeders must permanently identify their breeding stock by a tattoo, microchip, or DNA profile.

The United Kingdom also uses a Pet Passport system for dogs traveling out of the country under which microchipping is a requirement. For more information about the specifics of this program see www.gov.uk/take-pet-abroad.

Chapter 2 – Buying a Tibetan Mastiff

Are You Working With a Bad Breeder?

Clearly no animal lover wants to support the activities of a puppy mill. During your talks with breeders, beware of some of the following warning signs that the kennel in question is not reputable or following good practices.

- Reluctance or refusal to allow you to visit the kennel in person or excluding parts of the facility from an agreed upon tour for vague or implausible reasons. You may get the sense that you are being shown only a "staged" area of the facility.

- Offering to sell puppies sight unseen with little to no evaluation of your suitability as a "parent." If you get the feeling that you'll get a dog no matter what you say or do, something is definitely not right.

- Kennels that, upon examination, seem crowded and have a definite odor. Also be suspicious if the animals seem apprehensive and nervous. There are many conditions, including kennel cough that spread rapidly in over-crowded conditions. It is highly likely that any puppy raised under such circumstances will have health problems.

- Not being allowed to meet the puppies' parents or to see their photos and health records. While sires and dams are not always housed at the same kennel, you should be able to get information about them, including contact details for the kennel at which the animal is housed.

Chapter 2 – Buying a Tibetan Mastiff

- Inability to prove membership in any kennel club, to supply registration numbers, or otherwise to prove in a verifiable fashion ancestry extending back three generations.

- Dodgy answers in regard to health records for the puppies, or assurances that you will receive the information "later." In fact, a range of excuse may be supplied, including things like, "the vet retired" or "they just moved the office and the records aren't available yet." Beware all such spurious stories!

- Claims that there are no genetic health problems associated with the breed and no need for any kind of health screenings to be performed or that health screens have been performed and are 100% conclusive.

- Asserting that the puppy has been microchipped but lacking a scanner to prove that the identification number on the chip and on that on the bill of sale match.

- No clearly defined health guarantee with policies for the responsibility of each party if a health problem does arise. Be particularly suspicious if you're told there's absolutely no reason for the puppy to be evaluated by a veterinarian.

- Refusal to provide a signed bill of sale or claiming one will be provided later. If you have no bill of sale, the "breeder" can claim never to have seen you before. That is provided you can even locate them again in the event you have a complaint!

The only goal of a puppy mill is to spend as little as possible while producing multiple litters of puppies for profit. This means dogs are often being raised in horrific conditions, with no thought to quality healthcare or long-term behavior. Genetic abnormalities due to inbreeding are hugely problematic under these circumstances.

If you cannot visit the kennel where the puppies are offered for sale, or evaluate it by other means that technology makes available to you, and if you are not given complete genetic and health related information about the dog *do not do business with the kennel in question*. Move on!

Chapter 3 – Is This The Right Dog For Me?

Rare "objects" of all type attract some people. There's an allure to owning something no one else has. This desire easily extends to rare dog breeds, but the Tibetan Mastiff is a strong, independent living creature with a unique disposition and temperament. They are *not* the right dogs for just anyone.

If trained properly, the Tibetan Mastiff can be a superb and well-adjusted companion. However, owners with no understanding of the breed and who do not dedicate themselves to creating a sound relationship with the animal will face serious problems.

Do not take these statements lightly. Carefully and objectively evaluate the suitability of your circumstances as a proper Tibetan Mastiff home *BEFORE* adopting.

Chapter 3 – Is This The Right Dog For Me?

The Tibetan Mastiff's Personality

Breed standards are not necessarily the most insightful descriptions of a dog's personality, yet in this instance, there are two key words in that document: aloof and protective.

You may well read, however (and it is true) that the Tibetan Mastiff is an extremely loyal family dog with an affinity for other dogs and children (with proper adult supervision).

These qualities reflect the highly specific existence lived by these ancient dogs in their Tibetan homeland. However, nothing about that unique landscape and lifestyle prepares the breed for coping in the modern world, especially in Western cultures.

Instinct to Protect

Instincts as strongly engrained as those present in the Tibetan Mastiff cannot be erased quickly no matter how carefully planned a breeding program might be.

As a naturally occurring breed, survival of the fittest had a real and compelling role in making the Tibetan Mastiff the dog it is today. In the wrong setting, the consequences of those natural urges can be both problematic and potentially dangerous.

A Tibetan Mastiff needs guidance from a devoted master to understand what is required of him in his environment. This is a stubborn, but intelligent animal. He is hard wired as a guardian to the point of single mindedness. Once an idea is in the mind of this dog, he will act on it.

The Tibetan Mastiff continues to this day to work in that capacity in his native land, so this genetic imperative is still alive and well in the breed.

Independent Decision Maker

The Tibetan Mastiff's nature is primitive, but his mind is honed to his purpose as a nocturnal sentinel. He is an independent decision maker with a vivid memory and the physical strength and capabilities to execute any plan he devises.

A bored Tibetan Mastiff is an engine of destruction, easily chewing his way right through wood doors or similar impediments. This is not necessarily "bad" behavior. The dog may be trying to get out to go on his patrol "rounds," or he may decide he's identified an intruder with which he must deal.

Regardless, well-made fences that cannot be jumped, climbed, or tunneled under are essential with this breed. I'm not talking about average backyard fences. From a sitting position, some Tibetan Mastiff's can easily jump a six-foot (1.8 meter) fence of higher.

In a home, the dog will find a quiet post from which he can watch his surroundings. His presence will be kindly and watchful to the point of hypervigilance. The bond a Tibetan Mastiff forms with his owner is deep and trusting. This is a

Chapter 3 – Is This The Right Dog For Me?

dog capable of real affection and unusually devoted companionship.

Regular visitors to the house will be accepted when introduced carefully and when the dog is praised and encouraged for accepting and categorizing them as "no threat." The sooner in a dog's life these introductions can be made, the better.

However, the same dog in his own quarters, or kept outside in a yard will go to work protecting the area and posing a considerable threat to anyone who enters the space, especially strangers. It may be necessary to make modifications to your home and to your comings and goings to address this fact.

Tibetan Mastiffs should not just be placed in a yard and left to be guardians. They are easily bored, and they do get lonely. They are deeply devoted to their charges, whether those are people or animals. A Tibetan mastiff wants to be with the things he knows.

Training Considerations

Training is no simple matter with these dogs, and they are certainly not the right animals for first-time owners. Tibetan Mastiffs are quite capable of independent thought and must respect the person working with them.

Initial obedience training tends to go well with this breed until they bore of the repetitive tasks and begin to crave greater challenges.

Chapter 3 – Is This The Right Dog For Me?

It's never an issue of the Mastiff forgetting what he's learned, but rather of his wiliness to do it yet *again*. Forget about making him do anything he doesn't want to do.

Because puppies grow very quickly, Tibetan Mastiffs must be taught territorial boundaries early in life and their human owners must clearly be the "alpha" in the relationship. Good manners and behavior coupled with well-defined pack order is essential with these dogs.

> The leader of the pack, the alpha, dominates the other members and makes decisions for the group. Often there is both an alpha male and alpha female. All other subordinate members have their own place. In the home, you and your family are the pack. You must establish yourself as the alpha. If you don't the dog will take the responsibility from you and become the one in charge.

As if all of this were not complicated and challenging enough, the Tibetan Mastiff's bark has been described as the voice of an ancient copper gong. Until you've heard it, the deep resonance cannot be described adequately.

The sound is deep and sonorous, but unfortunately because they have worked the "night shift" for thousands of years, Tibetan Mastiffs have a tendency to literally bellow at night – hardly a good fit for an urban neighborhood.

Generally if a dog is kept indoors at night and schooled early on about inappropriate barking, this behavior can be controlled, but if a Tibetan Mastiff thinks he needs to "tell" you something, he will.

Chapter 3 – Is This The Right Dog For Me?

Physical Characteristics

The powerful Tibetan Mastiff is clearly massive in size, but he is also well built. His demeanor conveys seriousness to the point of solemnity, yet there is something benign and almost kind in his expression.

The broad skull rests on an arched neck ringed by a thick mane of hair. Wide, open nostrils sit prominently in the generous muzzle, an adaptation to the rarified air of a high altitude life.

Types of Tibetan Mastiff?

Often there are two types of the breed discussed. The "monastery" type (Tsang-khyi) is generally heavier and taller with bigger bones and more prominent facial wrinkles as opposed to the "nomad" (Do-khyi).

Chapter 3 – Is This The Right Dog For Me?

Since both can be present in one litter, however, there's considerable debate about the heavier, larger pups (which are rare) actually representing a different "kind" of Tibetan Mastiff.

Body Conformation and Size

In conformation, the Tibetan Mastiff's body is slightly longer than the dog is high at the shoulder. The muscular hindquarters are powerful and the feet are adapted to moving over snow-covered landscapes making for a dog far more agile and nimble than his size might suggest.

Cat-like in their shape, the feet are heavily feathered between the toes, which are often webbed. The combinations essentially equips the Tibetan Mastiff with snowshoes.

According to the American Kennel Club standard, females should stand at least 24 inches (61 cm) at the shoulder, with males measuring a minimum 26 inches (66 cm). The standard doesn't specify a weight, but since most individuals far exceed the lowest accepted heights, weights range from 100-160 lbs. / 45.36-72.57 kg).

Coat and Colors

Males have heavier coats, but both genders will experience severe shedding during warm weather. A heavy and wooly undercoat lies beneath the long topcoat. Overall the hair is silky, hard, and straight with no curl and stands off from the body.

Chapter 3 – Is This The Right Dog For Me?

The thick mane on the neck and shoulders is defensive in nature, protecting this vulnerable region of the body from attack. The highly placed tail curls over the back and shows good feathering.

Permitted colors range from gold to a deep, rich black. Tan markings above the eyes may be present in Tibetan Mastiffs that are black, gray, or blue. These animals are highly prized in Tibet where they are called "four eyes."

Such dogs are believed to have the ability to detect evil in advance. It's possible for a Tibetan Mastiff to have a white star on the chest, but it should not be large. Again, this marking is valued in Tibet as a sign of a brave heart. Some white on the feet is also permissible, but should not appear anywhere else on the body.

The dogs rarely require bathing since to do so would strip the coat of its natural oils.

Health Considerations

Not surprising due to the harshness of the conditions in their native land, Tibetan Mastiffs are hardy by nature. The major genetic issues that surface in the breed (which I will discuss at greater length in the chapter on health) are:

- **Entropion**, a condition in which the eyelids turn inward causing the eyelashes to press against and irritate or scratch the cornea of the eye. (Ectropion is also common and occurs when the eyelids torn outward.)

- **Canine Inherited Demyelinative Neuropathy (CIDN)**, a condition of the peripheral nervous system that causes the hindquarters to weaken at around six weeks of age progressing to complete paralysis over a period of weeks.

- **Hip and elbow dysplasia**, which is common in many large dog breeds. The problem stems from malformation of the ball and socket joints leading to an impaired gait, arthritis, and ongoing pain. This issue is exacerbated by obesity.

Thankfully, the concerted efforts of dedicated breeders have lessened the prevalence of these conditions, but there are no guarantees that a genetic issue will not surface in any line of dogs. Do not believe the assertions of breeders who claim their dogs could *never* present with such issues.

Serious Pre-Adoption Considerations

Given the highly specialized nature and history of the Tibetan Mastiff breed, it's important to carefully weigh a number of factors prior to adoption.

- The Tibetan Mastiff is not a "guard dog" per se in the way you would think of other breeds fulfilling this function. The most highly regarded guard dogs are the Bull Mastiff, Doberman Pinscher, Rottweiler, Komodor, Puli, Giant Schnauzer, German Shepherd, Rhodesian Ridgeback, Kuvasz, and Staffordshire Terrier.

Chapter 3 – Is This The Right Dog For Me?

- The Tibetan Mastiff should be considered a "guardian" breed. The dogs actually cannot be trained successfully to attack. Their job is to intimidate and scare off intruders. They can and have harmed intruders of all types, but that is not their primary function.

- You cannot necessarily control what a Tibetan Mastiff regards as a threat. If you cannot deal with destruction to your home and property by a dog that *thinks* he's doing his job, this is not the breed for you. Tibetan Mastiffs have even been known to damage parked vehicles they thought were invading their space.

- The breed grows quickly but matures slowly, so you are looking at a protracted puppyhood of several years. If you've raised a normal sized puppy, you know how challenging their behavior can be. Imagine that in a Tibetan Mastiff!

- The breed requires the companionship of its owners. The dog will become deeply attached to you. Are you prepared to fulfill that emotional need or deal with the destructive consequences of a bored and unhappy dog?

- Tibetan Mastiffs have been bred to be independent thinkers that can make decisions without the input of their humans. A dog guarding a flock in the field cannot wait for his master's command. Can you live with a dog that may well think it has a better

Chapter 3 – Is This The Right Dog For Me?

"answer" than yours to the current "problem" or "threat" at hand? Tibetan Mastiffs can be incredibly stubborn and single minded.

- When Tibetan Mastiffs are surrendered to rescues or given over to new homes the primary reasons cited are excessive barking at night, escapes due to boredom, destructive behavior, dominance over other animals, and over-protective behavior. Know these things in advance and think carefully before you adopt one of these dogs!

- Tibetan Mastiffs are highly individualistic. You cannot treat them like any other breed of dog, nor can you expect that your Mastiff will behave like a dog owned by another person. These dogs must be dealt with on a case-by-case basis.

- It is highly likely that to successful integrate a Tibetan Mastiff into your life you will need to alter the physical characteristics of your home, change your lifestyle, and work with a professional trainer. If you're not prepared to do these things – and to pay for them – this is not the breed for you.

For all these cautions, understand that the Tibetan Mastiff's spirit is so special and sensitive as to be described as magical. If that spirit is broken by boredom, loneliness, or mistreatment, you will have an angry, depressed dog on your hands with the physical ability to act out in impressive and highly destructive ways.

Chapter 3 – Is This The Right Dog For Me?

Tibetan Mastiffs need a tie of mutual affection, respect, and cooperation with their masters. If you cannot meet the emotional needs of these remarkable animals, do not adopt one.

With any breed, considering all its abilities and issue of temperament in advance is a critical aspect of adoption, but I cannot stress strongly enough that for the Tibetan Mastiff, this level of intentional foresight is *critical*.

Chapter 4 – Caring for Your Tibetan Mastiff

Clearly one of the first things prospective owners consider when they look at a Tibetan Mastiff is how they will ever afford to feed such a large dog. Surprising, this breed eats very little. Remember that these dogs evolved and lived in a sparse and harsh landscape. With this breed, housing and training considerations are actually more difficult to manage than diet.

Managing Your Dog's Diet

Tibetan Mastiff puppies grow rapidly, and like all dogs require a high-quality diet. One of the greatest nutritional problems with this breed are owners who allow young dogs to put on too much weight, which can seriously damage their development at a time when they are experiencing fundamental bone growth.

Weight management is equally important for adults, however, especially in the interest of avoiding joint-related health issues. Although as a breed these dogs do not tend to overeat, any companion animal can develop a taste for an inappropriate amount of food or treats if given the chance.

The tendency to be moderate eaters is again a consequence of the Tibetan Mastiff's development in a sparse landscape. Interesting, both sexes will regurgitate food to be fed to puppies. This partially digested material is still nutrient rich and therefore beneficial for the young dogs.

Overall, a low-protein diet is better for Tibetan Mastiffs. They have the ability to completely absorb all the nutrients present in their food and thus produce a much smaller amount of fecal matter than other dogs of comparable size.

Selecting Food for Your Dog

Always read the label of any food you are considering giving to your Tibetan Mastiff. Dry foods often contain fillers like soybean, corn or rice. Whatever is listed first on the label is the main ingredient, with the next most prevalent ingredients listed in descending order.

Dry foods that list meat or fish as a main ingredient are of a higher quality and offer more nutritional value, but they do tend to be more expensive. Larger breeds like the Tibetan Mastiff (regardless of this dog's relatively low food consumption) still eat more than smaller breeds. Thus, dry foods work very well with big dogs.

You can mix dry and wet foods in your dog's diet to ensure the animal is appropriately hydrated, and in the interest of variety. Wet food can also be used as a "treat."

Adding a splash of water to a Tibetan Mastiff's dry food is a good idea, especially on days that are hot and dry or very cold. The addition of the water can help to prevent bloat by making the dog slow down while eating.

Nutritional Transitions

A primary aspect of dietary management for any dog breed are those times with nutrition should be transitioned to a new level, for instance the change from puppy to adult food, or adult to a senior formula.

There are also times when a food you have been using is no longer available, or a superior product comes on the market and you are desirous of making a change.

The best policy to follow under these circumstances is to make the change gradually over the period of about a week, mixing the new food in with the old in slowly increasing increments until the switch over is complete.

A rapid alteration in your pet's diet will likely cause gastrointestinal upset to the point that an already picky eater may begin to refuse food. Although cat's have a well-known reputation for being finicky eaters, dogs are just as capable of this kind of maddening reaction to food they find "unacceptable" for reasons that may only make sense to the dog himself.

A Puppy's Diet

By the time you adopt a Tibetan Mastiff puppy, it should already be weaned from its mother's milk. When you take over supervising the dog's nutrition for the remainder of the first year of its life, you are overseeing a critical developmental phase during which the dog's skeletal and muscular structure becomes fully formed.

Poor diet and inadequate exercise during these months can cause health problems that will plague the dog for the rest of its life. Thankfully there are many high-quality commercial foods formulated specifically for growing puppies.

An Adult Diet

The adult diet for the Tibetan Mastiff is designed for maintenance and continued physical development. A puppy will reach its full height within a year, but physical growth continues until age 2-3, with some dogs only gaining full maturity at four years old.

Generally by 10-11 months a dog can be put on an adult formula food. Gauge your dog's weight by making certain the animal has a clearly visible "waist" and a slight layer of fat over the ribs. Obesity can greatly decrease a dog's lifespan.

Chapter 4 – Caring for Your Tibetan Mastiff

Maintain the same feeding schedule you established for the dog while he was a puppy. By this time your Tibetan Mastiff will be fully housebroken, but these dogs still like their routine and regular mealtimes will help you to keep track of how much your pet is eating.

A Senior Diet

A Tibetan Mastiff qualifies as a senior once it has attained 7 years of age, even though the breed can easily live in excess of 14 years. As seniors, this breed can metabolize more protein than in the puppy or adult stages of life.

Discuss required levels of protein with your veterinarian, and explore the potential of moving to a food formulated specifically for seniors. All dogs age differently, and your vet may not recommend this dietary change exactly on "schedule." The regular adult diet may continue for several years, but in smaller portions with as many as four feedings per day to facilitate easier digestion and as a precaution against dangerous episodes of bloat.

Weight control is even more important in a dog's senior years as this is also the stage of life when arthritis may begin to develop.

Decreased activity coupled with obesity can lead to joint degeneration, which is already a genetic possibility with the Tibetan Mastiff.

Feeding Schedules

Beginning when your Tibetan Mastiff is a puppy, the dog should be fed at the same time each day and in the same place. This is important to establish a daily routine to which the dog will respond well and around which proper housebreaking will focus. So long as your dog eats on schedule, he should also do his "business" on schedule.

Both puppies and adults should be fed three times a day with limited or no exercise an hour before or after meals. This is a precaution against bloat. Tibetan Mastiffs should not be allowed to free feed for the same reason, and in the interest of weight control.

The Danger of Bloat

Although bloat is not necessarily more common with the Tibetan Mastiff, the condition can be an issue with all large dog breeds, especially those with deep chests. Bloat can be caused by:

Chapter 4 – Caring for Your Tibetan Mastiff

- swallowing air while exercising
- gulping food and/or water
- exercising too soon before or after meals
- stress
- over-excitement at mealtime

Affected dogs suffer a painful twisting of the stomach that prevents food from exiting the organ while constricting the blood vessels. As gas builds up, toxins simultaneously flood the bloodstream causing shock and ultimately death. Symptoms include:

- crying out in pain
- dry heaving
- straining while attempting to defecate
- a refusal to walk or lie down
- hardening of the abdomen
- sensitivity of the abdomen to touch

The best way to prevent bloat is to limit the dog's activity before and after meals, to decrease the size of the portions offered while increasing the frequency of feedings, and to keep the animal as calm as possible while it is eating.

Specific Dietary Cautions

In picking a puppy's food, select a product that has less than 12% calcium content. Too much calcium can actually hamper proper skeletal development and predispose the dog to joint problems. Never supplement a puppy's diet

Chapter 4 – Caring for Your Tibetan Mastiff

with additional calcium beyond that which is already present in the food you purchase.

Other specific dietary cautions of which you should be aware include:

- Avoid giving your dog any milk other than goat's milk. Dogs do not tolerate cow's milk well because they don't have enough of the needed enzymes to digest lactose.

- Don't add raw eggs to your dog's food in the mistaken belief that it will make the animal's coat shiny. Eating raw eggs causes dogs to become biotin deficient, which can lead to anemia, dryness of the coat, and skin lesions.

- Table scraps should be avoided in the interest of weight management, but it is especially important not to let your pet eat highly seasoned of very fatty foods, which will lead to serious stomach upset.

- Be extremely cautious when offering raw meat to your pet. Make sure the meat is absolutely fresh and is only given as a very small part of a well-balanced diet.

- Do not give your dog large amounts of raw liver, which can cause Vitamin A toxicity. An overabundance of Vitamin A can lead to loss of appetite, constipation, the formation of bone spurs, stiffness, limping, weakness, weight loss, and overall lethargy.

A well-balanced commercial diet will have more than enough Vitamin A for your pet – but not too much.

- Avoid soft bones like those from chicken or pork. They splinter easily and can lacerate the dog's mouth, throat, stomach, and intestines. Only large raw beef knuckle or leg bones are appropriate.

Be especially vigilant about chocolate, no matter how small the amount, including any treat that advertises chocolate flavor or that is made of carob. These latter items are not dangerous in and of themselves, but they encourage the dog in the future to go after the real stuff, which is highly toxic.

One ounce of chocolate is enough to poison a 30 lb. / 13.6 kg dog. Cocoa beans contain the methylxanthine theobromine, which dogs metabolize slowly. It is damaging to the heart, kidneys, and central nervous system. Semi-sweet and dark chocolate is even more dangerous than milk chocolate, and baking chocolate and cocoa mix are the most toxic of all the chocolate variants.

Other toxic "people foods" include grapes, raisins, nuts, onions, and garlic.

Every dog enjoys a treat, and special tidbits are quite useful as positive reinforcement during training routines, but these items should be nutritious and specifically formulated for dogs. You can also use small pieces of cooked chicken or dried liver.

Avoid Popular Rawhide Chews

Although rawhide chew toys are especially popular for large, aggressive chewers like the Tibetan Mastiff, they present a choking hazard and can cause intestinal blockage. Dogs chew the material until it becomes a soft, wet mass, which they often swallow.

Additionally, rawhide toys made in foreign countries may contain anything from lead to arsenic and even be a source of the Salmonella bacilli. Typically the foreign-made chews are the cheapest, so it you insist on getting these toys for your pet, buy the more expensive items and supervise your dog, removing the chew before it softens.

It is true that chewing on rawhide cleans your pet's teeth, and the toys can distract the dog from attacking less appropriate targets like the living room sofa. Other

Chapter 4 – Caring for Your Tibetan Mastiff

chewing options include large beef bones and animal hooves.

The Importance of Clean Water

All dogs need a constant supply of fresh, clean water. If you are housebreaking a puppy, you may want to monitor the animal's intake, otherwise, water should be available at all times.

During periods of extreme heat or when the animal has engaged in vigorous exercise, make sure the water bowl doesn't go dry. Expect increased intake under those circumstances, however, if a dog suddenly begins drinking large amounts of water for no apparent reason, a qualified veterinarian should evaluate your pet.

Never, however, allow your Tibetan Mastiff to gulp water, particularly at meal times. As discussed above, this behavior can contribute to gastric torsion or bloat, which is extremely dangerous and potentially fatal.

Exercising Your Tibetan Mastiff

Until a Tibetan Mastiff reaches one year of age, exercise should be limited. Puppies should not be taken on long walks, and they need ample rest between sessions of play. As they reach adulthood, the level of activity can be gradually increased.

A fully-grown animal can walk for miles a day, and will likely outlast you in the activity department.

Chapter 4 – Caring for Your Tibetan Mastiff

Regular walks not only keep your pet well exercised, but also serve to keep him interested and engaged. Remember that these dogs are active thinkers and easily subject to boredom. Do not, however, let your Tibetan Mastiff off its lead unless you are in a securely enclosed area. Never underestimate the power of your pet's guarding instinct.

Provide a fenced exercise yard for your pet, and police the area routinely. Mastiffs are great chewers, and will often escape through holes they've gnawed in their enclosures. The dogs are actually not attempting to run away, but rather fulfilling the instinctual urge to patrol their territory.

Coat Maintenance and Grooming

Establish a grooming routine with your Tibetan Mastiff puppy as soon as possible. Take your time, and get your animal accustomed to this activity in a stress-free and relaxed environment. The basic tools you will need include:

- large nail clippers
- large pin brush
- medium to fine metal comb
- dematting rake
- slicker brush

Although Tibetan Mastiffs have thick coats, they require nothing more than weekly brushing and combing to be kept free of mats and tangles.

Chapter 4 – Caring for Your Tibetan Mastiff

Start at the bottom of the legs and work upward, moving from the back of the body and going toward the front. Be sure to get all the way down to the skin, bringing your implement outward through the coat.

Use the dematting comb alone on small mats, but put baby powder on those that are medium sized. Rub the powder through the mat and then gently work it out with the slicker brush. The largest tangles will require use of the dematting rake.

The most common areas to find mats are behind the ears, in the feathering on the front and back legs, under the "arms," and in the tail plume.

Always work on any mats that are present before you begin to bathe your dog. If you let the mats get wet, they will "felt" and be much, much harder to remove.

Typically in the spring these dogs "blow coat," the term used to describe the shedding of the undercoat in large, profuse clumps. During this period, brush and comb your pet daily.

> ***Never clip or shear
> a Tibetan Mastiff
> during hot weather.***

Don't clip or shear your Tibetan Mastiff in the summer. You won't be doing your pet a favor at all! The dog's coat works as an insulator at all times of the year. It is as much a protection against heat as cold. Shearing a Tibetan Mastiff only *increases* the dog's risk for heat stroke.

Grooming as Preventive "Medicine"

In addition to keeping your pet aesthetically maintained, grooming is also an important part of preventive healthcare for your dog. It will afford you the chance to look for:

- hot spots
- tooth decay
- eye and ear infections
- eye and ear discharge
- parasites
- lumps, growths, and cuts
- embedded thorns and debris

For city dwelling dogs, check the pads for any substance like tar, gum, asphalt, or broken glass that may have become stuck to or embedded in the feet. Country dogs may pick up thorns, sticks, burrs, mold, or seeds.

Check a male dog's penile sheath and a female's vaginal opening for signs of infection, inflammation, or discharge.

Bathing Your Dog

Your Tibetan Mastiff will only need to be bathed a few times a year. Animals that are bathed too often will experience skin dryness from the removal of the natural oils present in their coat.

Chapter 4 – Caring for Your Tibetan Mastiff

Dogs react with varying degrees of enthusiasm to having a bath. Some enjoy the process and are cooperative; others must be wrestled into the tub resisting with every ounce of their strength, which with a Tibetan Mastiff is formidable!

Always have everything you need on hand and try to work in an area with a non-slip surface since water is likely to go everywhere – especially if your pet decides to stage a hasty exit.

It's greatly to your advantage to have a hose or shower spray with which to work. This will not only help you to get the animal completely wet, but also to remove all shampoo from the coat.

Use a shampoo specifically formulated for dogs. Human shampoos are too harsh and will dry out your pet's coat.

Start by wetting the coat thoroughly to the skin. Work the shampoo into the coat, keeping the lather away from the face (especially the eyes) and the ears.

Rinse just as thoroughly, still avoiding the face, eyes, and ears. Wrap the dog in a towel to get as much of the water out of the coat as possible. If the dog will allow it, use a blow dryer to speed up the process.

Keep your pet inside and out of any drafts until the animal is thoroughly dry.

Cleaning Your Dog's Ears

Although you should not allow your dog's ears to become wet, or let water run into the ear canal during a bath, you should monitor the condition of the ears to prevent a buildup of wax or an infestation of mites.

Check the inside of your Tibetan Mastiff's ears to make sure the skin looks pink and clean. There should be no accumulation of black tarry-looking wax, and no strong, yeast-like odor.

If debris is present and an odor, a vet should examine the animal. A swab will be taken to test the wax and if mites are present, a topic medication will cure up the infestation in a matter of days.

Never insert a cotton swab into your pet's ears as you could seriously damage the eardrum. Instead, use a cotton pad or cotton ball moistened with water or an ear cleaning solution to gently wipe the earflap clean. You can also use vinegar or hydrogen peroxide diluted with water.

Eye Care

While you are grooming your Tibetan Mastiff, look at the area around the eyes for soiling or for accumulated matter. Use a clean washcloth dampened with warm water to remove any build-up.

If staining is present, there are commercial eye cleaning solutions to remove the discoloration without irritating the eye.

If you see signs of a potential infection, a vet should examine the dog. These include, but are not limited to:

- excessive mucus
- redness, puffiness, or other indicators of irritation
- scabs
- constant runny discharge
- opacities in the eye

The sooner issues with the eye are detected and treated, the less likely the dog will be to lose part or all of its vision.

Dental Care

Approximately 80% of all companion canines will have some type of dental problem by age 2, with the percentage increasing with age. Proactive dental care at home is an important aspect of good husbandry for your Tibetan Mastiff.

The most commonly seen problem is a build-up of plaque, which can lead to gum disease, tooth infection, and potential tooth loss. If you look at your dog's teeth, you may be able to see black or yellow streaks of plaque.

Chapter 4 – Caring for Your Tibetan Mastiff

Additionally, bacteria originating in the mouth may spread to other parts of the body and contribute to the development of more serious illnesses.

You can obtain canine toothpaste from your vet, and try one of several methods to actually "brush" your pet's teeth. There are indeed dog toothbrushes that look not unlike our own, but have smaller heads. Another variation is a finger toothbrush with rubber bristles.

Many vets, however, say you can just use your bare finger and rub the paste around on your dog's teeth. Getting even some of the cleanser on the teeth is better than none at all. If your dog likes the flavor of the toothpaste, you clearly have a huge advantage.

The earlier you begin dental care with your Tibetan Mastiff puppy the better. Start slow and don't push the issue.

Chapter 4 – Caring for Your Tibetan Mastiff

Allow the dog to get used to being held and to having a brush or your finger inserted in its mouth.

If you are careful and diligent, you should be able to make regular dental care a conflict-free aspect of your pet's regular grooming routine.

It's also a good idea to offer your dog dental toys and dental cleansing treats and biscuits to help keep down the accumulation of plaque. From time to time the vet may recommend a full tooth cleaning.

You should be aware, however, that dogs must be under light anesthesia when this procedure is performed. Tibetan Mastiffs have a reputation for poor tolerance of anesthesia. Discuss this with your veterinarian in advance.

If the vet has no experience with this breed, he should consult with a colleague who has worked with these dogs before proceeding with the dental cleaning.

Nail Clipping or Grinding?

At least once a month, look at your dog's nails to see if clipping is required. If the animal routinely walks on rough, hard surfaces, this may not be a chore with which you have to deal often or at all. As a general rule of thumb, if the nails click when the dog moves across a hardwood or tile floor, a clipping is required.

In most cases you can use a simple set of "guillotine" nail clippers with handles like a pair of pliers to snip off the end of the nails when they grow too long. If the Tibetan Mastiff has been trained from an early age to tolerate nail clipping, all should be well, but some dogs simply won't put up with the feel of the clippers.

In those cases, a nail grinder is an alternate option. This tool employs a small, rotating sandpaper disc to take the nails down to a more appropriate length. Grinders also lessen the chance that you will cut into the quick of the nail, which is painful to the animal and will cause excessive bleeding.

It's a good idea to keep a styptic pencil or powder on hand in case you do cause a nail to bleed. Both will stop the flow quickly when applied to the end of the nail. If this happens, don't panic; just staunch the bleeding while speaking soothingly to the dog.

Neither suggested method – clippers or a grinder -- is "right" or "wrong." The choice is more a matter of what your Tibetan Mastiff best tolerates.

Anal Gland Maintenance

Dogs have glands located on either side of the anal vent that typically empty at the same time a bowel movement occurs. This is a function of the animal's scent marking, which defines his territory for himself and other dogs.

Sometimes, however, the anal glands fill up and become impacted, which causes considerable discomfort. In an attempt to open the glands, the dog will scoot across the ground or floor on their behinds. When this is the case, the anal glands need to be expressed so they will be open and functioning appropriately. I do not recommend assisting your dog with this chore.

The procedure isn't necessarily difficult, but owners tend to be tentative in their approach to the chore, communicating their nervousness to the dog and often increasing the pain of the condition. If the dog gets a negative association with having the glands expressed, future episodes will be much more difficult to address.

Professional groomers are experienced in performing this task, but unless your Tibetan Mastiff trusts the person, the dog may become aggressive. Typically, it's better to let your groomer attempt to handle anal gland issues first. If this proves impossible, or if there is a severe impaction, seek the assistance of your veterinarian.

Taking your dog to the vet may require the use of light anesthesia to prevent the animal from becoming aggressive in response to being handled in a very private area. Since Tibetan Mastiffs sometimes tolerate anesthesia poorly, discuss this fact with the vet before allowing the procedure to be performed.

Traveling with a Tibetan Mastiff

The degree to which your dog travels with you is completely dependent on the individual animal's reaction to being in the car.

Chapter 4 – Caring for Your Tibetan Mastiff

Desensitization early in life generally helps Tibetan Mastiffs to overcome travel-related anxiety, but some dogs suffer from motion sickness. When car travel is an absolute necessity, the animal may require medication.

At the very least, your dog will need to travel back and forth to the vet for annual checkups. Sometimes ginger snap cookies can help to ease the discomfort of carsickness.

Test your puppy by taking him on short car trips around the block, gradually increasing the distance according to the dog's comfort level. If he is a problem traveler, measure the distance to your vet and work on helping your dog tolerate a car ride of that duration with as little upset as possible.

Some Tibetan Mastiffs are born to hit the open road. For these dogs, your major concern is safety in a moving vehicle. Do not let your dog be loose in the car. This poses a dangerous distraction to the driver and increases the risk of fatal injury to the dog in the event of an automobile accident.

Get young puppies used to riding in a travel crate, especially one that can be secured in place with the seat belt. Due to the massive size of the Tibetan Mastiff, transition the dog to wearing a canine seatbelt, which is a modified form of harness attachable to the car's existing safety restraints.

Canine seatbelts are easily obtained through any major pet store or online and retail for less than $50 / £30.

When traveling with your dog, make sure you have everything the animal needs including his leash, water and food bowls, and bags to collect and discard feces.

It is important to keep all dogs leashed during stops while on trips, but even more vital for the Tibetan Mastiff given the dogs' strong protective instincts.

Never leave a dog inside a parked car. Not only is the animal at serious danger of suffering heat exhaustion during the warm months, but he is also a potential target for thieves.

A Tibetan Mastiff is certainly capable of defending himself, but the chances that the animal would be harmed during such an encounter are far too real to ever take such a risk.

Chapter 4 – Caring for Your Tibetan Mastiff

Boarding

Many kennels that board animals will not accept Tibetan Mastiffs because they do not have the room or do not understand how to manage the breed. These dogs need to be housed and fed separately so if you anticipate the need to board your pet, begin your search well in advance.

Visit each of the facilities you are considering and ask for a tour. Meet the staff and get a clear understanding of what services are offered and at what price. Specifically find out if anyone working there has prior experience around Tibetan Mastiffs. Do not let any staff members tell you they can handle any breed of dog. The Tibetan Mastiff isn't just any dog!

If you don't find a suitable kennel, talk to your vet and see if they either board dogs or can recommend other kennels. Regardless of where you board the dog, the facility will require proof of vaccinations and may ask to see other health records. The dog also will need proper identification.

Ideally you will have someone in your life with whom the dog has a rapport that can stay with your pet while you are away, but this is not like asking a friend to keep any other kind of dog. Your pet sitter would need to be in residence during your absence and be prepared to actually spend time with the Tibetan Mastiff.

Chapter 5 – Training Your Tibetan Mastiff

Your Tibetan Mastiff puppy should be 8-10 weeks of age at adoption. Coming to live with you is a new and potentially overwhelming experience. The dog is away from its mother and littermates, and has likely interacted with no people other than the breeder.

The Critical First Year

During the first two months the dog is with you, he will be eager to please and will be learning all the lessons that should form the foundation of his new life. This is a critical period, and one in which you have tremendous responsibility for shaping and training your new pet.

Following the initial two months of getting to know you and his new home, the dog will have about an 18-month

Chapter 5 – Training Your Tibetan Mastiff

window during which his good behavior can be reinforced and his manners refined. After that, the Tibetan Mastiff is a fully formed adult with ideas and opinions all his own.

Think of the puppy as what it is, a young and precocious child that must first understand basic, age-appropriate commands and routines. This is the phase of life where the dog should learn words like "down" or "off" if you don't want him on the furniture, for instance. Certainly as an all-purpose admonishment, your puppy should know the word "no."

As your puppy grows, there's more than enough time to introduce it to games and activities that will make his life – and yours – richer and more interesting. This isn't to say there won't be lots of play with a puppy in the house, but don't neglect to teach your new pet the fundamentals of good behavior either.

Raising and training a puppy should involve every person in the household. Each person present in the dog's life must know and enforce the rules that apply to the animal and use the same "command" words. This builds a consistent vocabulary for the dog, which is the only way you can realistically expect consistent responses from a Tibetan Mastiff or any other animal.

Dogs are pack animals with an innate desire to please their leader or "alpha." That should be you. Often in a dog's logic, the person the animal regards most highly and wants most to please is the one who dispenses the food.

This is why using small treats with verbal praise works so well to bond with and train a canine. Ultimately the positive words alone will be all that is needed to maintain desirable behaviors.

Dogs recognize and accept the social structure of the pack. Teaching a dog to behave as you want and praising the animal for doing well is proper discipline. Don't confuse discipline with punishment. One is positive and constructive; the other is negative and punitive.

> *Don't confuse discipline with punishment.*

Never mete out physical punishment to a puppy. Remember that Tibetan Mastiffs are unusually intelligent and bond strongly with their masters. If you are clearly displeased and show this with your voice and facial expression, the puppy will understand.

Also, don't use the dog's name when admonishing him. Reserve the use of his name for positive attention and reinforcement.

Crating and Containing Puppies

Before you bring your Tibetan Mastiff puppy home, decide where the dog's "home" inside the house will be. Don't give a puppy free run of the house. All puppies chew, but Tibetan Mastiff puppies are chewing *machines*.

Chapter 5 – Training Your Tibetan Mastiff

Often with puppies, using a crate as "home base" is extremely beneficial since it gives the little dog a sense of security, satisfies his need to establish territory, and assists with housebreaking.

Dogs will not soil the den where they sleep, so keeping the puppy crated at night and while you are away will aid in developing a regular schedule of outdoor breaks.

Once you've placed the dog in the crate for the night, even if it's in the corner of your bedroom, don't respond to pitiful whining or crying. The puppy will settle down after a few minutes.

Obviously the puppy shouldn't be confined in its crate for long periods of time. Instead, create one puppy-proof area for your young Tibetan Mastiff where you can be with the dog and supervise it carefully.

The kitchen is an excellent choice not only because the floor is washable, but also because the dog will be exposed to normal household activity and a good level of sounds. Secure the area with a baby gate or similar barrier. At this age, your pet won't be able to climb out. Enjoy it while it lasts!

Regardless of where you confine the puppy, make sure the dog can't get into any cabinets where cleaning supplies are kept, or pull on electrical cords. The latter not only present a danger of electrocution, but might also allow the dog to topple over a heavy household appliance or entertainment unit.

(Always make sure there are newspapers down just in case nature calls!)

The Difficulties of Adult Adoptions

Adopting an adult dog presents a whole different range of challenges. First, try to find out why the dog was given up for adoption. It is not unusual for Tibetan Mastiffs to be surrendered due to issues with "aggression." It's important, however, to try to discern exactly what is meant by the use of that word.

If the dog has received little training (or none) and his territorial and guardian tendencies are not well regulated, the transition to a new home will be rocky, even with the help of a knowledgeable professional trainer.

New rules are hard for all old dogs to accept, but the analytical and independent decision-making mind of a Tibetan Mastiff is even more resistant to changes for which the dog doesn't see a good reason. Never underestimate this breed's capacity for stubbornness.

With adult dogs you also have to carefully discover how they react to children, outsiders, and other animals. Tibetan Mastiffs are incredibly loyal family dogs and typically get along well with other dogs and even with cats. They do, however, have a completely unpredictable reaction to anyone or anything they regard as a "stranger."

Socialization in puppyhood is important for all breeds, but even more so for a Tibetan Mastiff, who must learn to look to his master for cues that will guide his reaction.

It is always best for the dog to be introduced to all regular visitors to your home as soon as possible so they become known entities. Clearly this is much more difficult when an adult is adopted and is a situation that must be handled with extreme caution.

Dogs Respond Well to Routine

In general, all dogs are creatures of habit. They thrive on routine and structure, but they don't react well to boredom.

Chapter 5 – Training Your Tibetan Mastiff

This is especially true of the Tibetan Mastiff. Because they were historically used as nocturnal guardians for flocks, households, and properties, these dogs are analytical in their assimilation of information and will act independently.

When they don't have enough stimulus to occupy their active thought processes, they find something to do – usually something you don't want them to do, and often something that is highly destructive, like chew their way through a door or a fence.

This capacity is a positive for the success of training endeavors, however. Interesting training sessions and varied activities are highly enjoyable for intelligent dogs like the Tibetan Mastiff and will positively contribute to their overall good behavior and responsiveness as companion animals.

Housebreaking: The First Important Routine

Young puppies have a lot of "business" to attend to every day. Often they must be taken out 8-12 times to avoid accidents. Be vigilant for signaling behavior like sniffing around the room or turning in small circles. Use your common sense. Take the dog out before and after naps, after meals, and after vigorous play sessions.

As the dog grows and becomes accustomed to his routine, the number of daily trips will drop to 6-8 per day by 6 months of age and then 5-7 at 8 months. Adults typically have to be taken out roughly four times: morning, afternoon, evening, and right before bedtime.

A Tibetan Mastiff is fairly easy to house train because of their high level of intelligence and fastidious natures. They have a tactile reaction to the process of house training, and will recognize by touch the surfaces on which they are given permission to eliminate.

If possible, create a small area in one corner of the yard that is covered in crushed stone. The dog will interpret the space as entirely "his" and you will have a much easier time cleaning up the space and removing feces.

This tendency of the breed also facilitates early paper training in the house with newspapers or puppy pads to avoid accidents. The dog will understand where it is and is not allowed to go in an emergency, but will still make the intuitive leap to what is acceptable when taken outdoors.

Each time a puppy relieves himself in the correct location, you should praise the dog to reinforce his good behavior. Be patient. Even the most well behaved young dogs have accidents, usually because they have so much excess energy and just get too excited.

Never "punish" a puppy for an accident. You'll only be setting back the progress of his training by confusing the dog. Instead, thoroughly clean the area with a specially formulated enzymatic cleaner like Nature's Miracle that will remove all traces of odor. Don't rely on regular household cleaners.

Without correct clean up, the dog will be attracted to the spot again and may interpret it as an acceptable location to urinate or defecate. If you witness the accident, say "no" in a stern voice and carry the dog outside. Even if the puppy is finished, you want to create the association in the dog's mind that "outside" is the bathroom.

Collars / Harnesses and Leads

Increasingly dog owners are leaning toward the use of harnesses over collars for controlling dogs of all sizes while on a lead. Although a traditional method, collars place undue stress on the dog's windpipe and can seriously harm an animal struggling to be free.

In buying harnesses, always bring at least two sizes home. Opt for the one that is snug, but not tight. You do not want the unit to constrict the dog's movements, but rather to serve as a secure point of attachment for the lead.

Puppies will do fine on a short 6' (1.8 meters) leash, but as your dog grows, invest in a heavy-duty retractable lead designed for use with large dogs. These leads are perfect for allowing your dog to get exercise in a park or field while still maintaining control of the animal.

Basic Training Exercises

The Tibetan Mastiff does best with one-on-one training that serves to bond him to his master. You may want to attend a training class without your dog in advance of the adoption to understand the primary goals of basic dog "education."

Chapter 5 – Training Your Tibetan Mastiff

After you have established a good working relationship with your new pet, you may both benefit from advanced classes with a trainer who has experience with this breed. Some of the fundamental exercises to master first include:

Sit

There are many methods to associate the command "sit" with the action in the mind of a dog. A particularly effective way is to put the dog in front of you with his lead attached.

Place a treat in the palm of your right hand and show it to the dog. Then, bring your hand up under his nose and slowly back to force the dog to tilt his head to follow the treat.

He'll either have to sit down or fall over. You may have to actually life your dog's chin until he sits, but as soon as he does, say "good dog" and give him the treat.

Chapter 5 – Training Your Tibetan Mastiff

Graduate to bringing the treat to the level of your waist and saying sit. This reinforces both the motion of your hand and the command itself as indicators of the desired behavior.

The sit command should be used at key times during the day, for instance instruct the dog to sit before giving him his food, or before the door is opened prior to an outing. This will help to promote calmer behavior at times when the dog might otherwise become unruly and overly excited.

Down

"Down" is a difficult position for a dog to assume because it indicates submission and potential danger. Begin this lesson with the puppy sitting to your left. Hold the leash with your left hand directly above the collar.

With your right hand, hold a treat at the end of the dog's nose and move your hand down and forward along the ground. Use the leash to stop the dog from lunging toward the food. Don't jerk the leash or do anything to panic the dog or make it feel threatened.

As the puppy goes into the down position, say "down," but do so gently. Make sure to keep the dog in the desired position for several seconds, keeping him down by pressing gently on his shoulders if he tries to stand too quickly. Never make the dog feel trapped.

Use an appropriate cue for the "release" (when the dog is allowed to stand up) like, "okay, good dog." Work on steadily increasing the amount of "down" time.

Stay

"Stay" should be a multi-purpose command applicable to both standing and sitting situations. Begin by having the dog sit on your left side. Hold the leash at the level of your waist. Let the dog know that you have a treat in your right hand.

With your right foot, step forward and say, "Stay." Turn and stand in front of the dog. Hold your right hand higher than your waist to keep the dog's attention until the animal will sit for a count of five. Return to your original position and reward your pet.

Continue to work on this routine until the dog will hold the stay position for at least a count of 30 seconds. After about a week, take two steps, and so on until you can walk the length of the training leash or farther without the dog moving.

Come

The "come" command should never be used as an admonishment or "punishment" with your dog. When you want to reprimand the animal, you should go to him.

The "come" command is a safety signal for your pet and your means of reliable recalling your pet no matter the situation. It should only be associated in the dog's mind with positive, pleasant, safe things.

When you want to reprimand the animal, you should go to him.

Reinforce the "come" command every single time a puppy moves toward you and always use his name. "Joe, come. Good boy!"

Practice this command under a variety of circumstances:

- on leash
- off leash
- when the dog is attentive
- when the dog is distracted

It's fine when your pet is leashed to give the lead a mild jerk if the dog doesn't respond or seems confused about what you want. The tug only indicates direction, and should not be forceful.

Heel

Never allow a dog on a lead to pull or yank you down the street. It's annoying with any breed, but a fully-grown Tibetan Mastiff is unbelievably strong. You must always be in charge of the pace and direction.

When teaching a dog to heel, keep the dog on your left side and step off with your left foot. Begin the motion with the word, "Heel." Keep the leash loose, but when the dog pulls ahead, bring him back, tell him to sit, and only begin again after he has been still for several seconds.

When he will step off correctly and stay by your side, stop, tell the dog to sit, and calmly praise him when he complies. Don't be overly enthusiastic, or the dog will assume the lesson is over.

Continue to repeat this exercise by increasing the number of steps you take with the dog walking correctly beside you. When you're finished for the day, have the dog sit a longer period of time, and then tell him, "Okay," and praise him for doing a good job. This will signal to your pet that the lesson is over.

Combining the commands to heel, sit, and stay can be very taxing on a dog, especially a young puppy, so make sure you follow this more difficult training exercise with a lot of free time to run and play. Think of this as letting your dog out for "recess."

Cutting Back on the Treats as Rewards

As your dog becomes more proficient at the basic obedience commands or any more complex lessons you've taught your pet, begin to decrease the number of treats given as rewards while remaining consistent with your praise. If you keep up the treat reward system, you'll have an overweight dog on your hands in no time.

Remember, you are working with an animal that has a genetic drive to please the leader of his "pack." In time, praise alone should be sufficient to maintain the dog's good behavior. Only return to the routine of treats when you are teaching your pet a new command or lesson.

Chapter 5 – Training Your Tibetan Mastiff

Attending Classes or Obtaining a Trainer

Young Tibetan Mastiffs can be headstrong dogs. Remember that the breed grows very quickly, but matures slowly. Just like toddlers, all puppies go through a stage when they are "selectively deaf" and will test you by seeming not to hear your commands or by rebelling outright.

If you have established yourself as the pack leader, you will be able to get past this stage with your dog on your own. Training a Tibetan Mastiffs requires perseverance, consistency, and a great deal of patience.

Don't be upset with yourself or with your dog if you need the help of a professional trainer either in a class setting or through one-on-one lessons. The important thing is that your dog *is* properly trained.

You must, however, find a trainer who has experience with this breed and its unique temperament and territorial instinct. Always interview potential instructors before signing up to work with the person, and if possible, arrange to see them in action with other dogs.

Taking your puppy to an obedience class does have the advantage of getting your pet used to the distraction and stimulus of being around other people and dogs. This type of socialization is important for any young dog, but is crucial for a Tibetan Mastiff.

Remember that you must reinforce the dog's good habits throughout your pet's life. No matter how well a dog learns

Chapter 5 – Training Your Tibetan Mastiff

the correct commands and behaviors with a trainer, your pet will become lax and do as he pleases if you let him get away with it.

This is not only a function of the Tibetan Mastiff's innate obstinate streak, but also his native intelligence and independence decision-making ability. To some extent, training this breed is really a matter of striking a functional deal with a dog that is more partner than pet.

Chapter 6 – Tibetan Mastiff Health

Preventive healthcare is one of the most important aspects of responsible canine husbandry. No one will ever know your dog better than you do, or be a more effective advocate for his health needs throughout his life.

Being well cared for not only will make your dog happier and better behaved, it will also extend his lifespan.

Adopting a Healthy Dog

There is no way to absolutely guarantee that any puppy will be free of health problems or genetic issues, but clearly there are steps you can and should take to ensure you are adopting a healthy Tibetan Mastiff puppy.

Working with a reputable breeder from a well-established kennel is your best safeguard. Reviewing the health records of the puppy's parents is an important part of the adoption process, as is obtaining any existing medical records for the puppy itself.

If the dogs at the kennel have been screened for specific genetic conditions, ask to see documentation of the testing and an explanation of the results. Do not believe any claims regarding testing if there is no documented proof.

There are only a few disorders for which these kinds of screenings can be performed, and these do *NOT* include hip dysplasia, cataracts, epilepsy, or hypertrophic cardiomyopathy.

Although temperament is not a matter of healthcare per se, many Tibetan Mastiffs are euthanized annually because their aggressive tendencies create problems the owners cannot control over overcome.

Assessing a predisposition for aggression in a genetic line while difficult is still important to at least attempt. This is one reason why you should ask for references and follow up on those contacts when adopting a Tibetan Mastiff puppy. Always try to find out how dogs from the kennel have done living with their new families.

Early Medical Care

Even before you bring your puppy home, some important healthcare measures should already have been performed.

Chapter 6 – Tibetan Mastiff Health

At about two weeks of age, routine measures are taken to make sure puppies are free of both internal and external parasites (worms and/or fleas).

The recommended course of vaccinations starts at 6-8 weeks, although, as will be discussed shortly, this can be a matter of some debate.

Regardless of where the dog is living, a general health evaluation at six months is standard. This check-up includes a dental evaluation, the instigation of a life-long program of heartworm prevention, and the decision to spay or neuter the animal.

Dental Health

Taking care of your dog's dental health is much more important than you might think and should also start as early in the dog's life as possible. By four years of age, most companion canines are already showing signs of periodontal disease.

Regular tooth cleanings, brushing at home, and the use of dental chews and toys can greatly reduce this risk. Dental problems cause bad breath, but also lead to gum disease. Signs of potential dental problems include the following and require evaluation by a qualified veterinarian:

- Loose, broken, or missing teeth.
- Changes in eating behavior that might indicate pain or infection.
- Inflamed, swollen, or bleeding gums.

Chapter 6 – Tibetan Mastiff Health

- Bad breath.
- Drooling with or without blood present.
- Yellowing of the teeth.

From your first meeting with the veterinarian, discuss the best ways to keep your Tibetan Mastiff's teeth in good condition.

Finding A Good Veterinarian

Selecting a qualified veterinarian is one of the most important decisions you will ever make to support your pet's long-term wellbeing. Vets are incredibly all-purpose caregivers in a dog's life, serving the range of needs from pediatric to elder care.

Over the course of your dog's life, the vet will make recommendations based on your pet's ongoing record of medical information and required diagnostic testing. The vet will have a copy of all records from required treatments by specialists as well as any emergency situations that might arise.

You want a vet that is an advocate both for your dog, but also your ally in understanding the often-confusing details of medical care. The best vets have a good "bed side" manner that extends both to the animal and the human. You rely on your vet to give you the information you need to make good choices on your dog's behalf.

Depending on the owner's area of comfort, the most important quality in a vet may be compassionate understanding or superb diagnostic insight. Ideally, you will find a working professional with both these qualities (and more), and one who has access to state-of-the-art equipment.

It's also important to know when the vet clinic is open and where you would go or be sent in an emergency.

- What is the proximity of the facility to your home?

- Will the vet make house calls if necessary?

- Will one vet treat your dog consistently or will other doctors at the clinic treat your pet?

- Does the doctor you are considering have specific experience with the Tibetan Mastiff breed?

Think of your vet as your dog's primary care physician, but at the same time realize that veterinary medicine is now highly diversified. Ask if the vet maintains ongoing relationships for referrals to surgeons, ophthalmologists, internists, cardiologists, oncologists, neurologists, and other specialists.

Make a short list of potential clinics in your area and visit each one for the express purpose of seeing the facility and meeting the vet. Make a regular appointment, but explain why you are coming in and that you are perfectly willing to pay the regular fee for an office visit. If an office objects to a paid visit for the purpose of an interview, strike that facility off your list and move on.

When you do visit a clinic, have all of your questions prepared in writing before you arrive. Vets are busy people. Get the information you need and don't waste anyone's time.

Only when you feel you've found a good fit for your needs and those of your dog should you make an appointment to take your pet into the clinic for an initial evaluation.

Annual Vet Visits

Even if your pet is completely healthy and no vaccinations are required, annual vet visits are important. Having an ongoing relationship with a veterinary professional allows for a coordinated program of healthcare and for subtle changes over time to be checked against baseline measurements.

This approach to routine healthcare will also effectively track the transitional phases in your dog's life of which you might otherwise not be fully aware. For instance, Tibetan Mastiffs do not reach full maturity until age 3-4, but by year 7 they are already considered senior dogs.

Typically, these life transitions pass with no particular fanfare in well cared for dogs, but thorough medical records and regular check-ups are essential to spot and address any problems early before more serious illnesses can develop.

Due to the risk of heart disease later in life, particularly hypertrophic cardiomyopathy, it is generally best for elderly Tibetan Mastiffs (age 7 or more) to see the vet twice a year. If any cardiac abnormalities have been detected, annual laboratory screening and electrocardiograms may also be required.

Most health problems that arise with aging dogs can be managed with good quality of life for your pet, including cancer, diabetes, arthritis and even cognitive dysfunction or "doggie dementia."

Vaccinations

Thanks to advances in veterinary medicine, it is now possible to vaccinate your dog against a number of infectious diseases. The major ones are listed and described below.

Rabies

Vaccination against the viral disease rabies, which can devastate animals and humans, is so important it is a legal requirement in all 50 states, the Canadian provinces, the United Kingdom, and the European Union.

This vaccination is not optional, and pet owners must be able to provide proof that the shot has been given annually, typically by displaying tags on the dog's collar or harness.

Parvovirus

There are four strains of the parvovirus, which is a potentially life threatening and highly contagious illness among dogs. Even people working with infected animals can pass the disease on to other canines.

Symptoms include lethargy, loss of appetite, severe vomiting, and bloody diarrhea. The condition often leads to fatal dehydration
The available parvovirus vaccines may protect against one or more of the identified variations of the disease.

Distemper

Distemper is a severe and life-threatening viral disease often contracted by young puppies. There is no cure. It is spread in the air or by contact between affected individuals.

Dogs with distemper are lethargic and have no appetite. Coughing, vomiting, and diarrhea are all present. In the later stages of the disease, the animal's nervous system is compromised and seizure activity will likely be present.

Young dogs may gain protection from the human measles vaccine since the two viruses are related. These shots are typically administered at age 4-10 weeks.

(This condition should not be confused with "kennel cough," which is a form of bronchitis.)

Kennel Cough

The infectious respiratory disease tracheobronchitis is commonly referred to as kennel cough. Puppies, age 6 weeks to 6 months are particularly vulnerable, however surviving a bout of the disease does not convey future immunity. Dogs of any age can suffer from kennel cough.

Multiple infectious agents can be responsible including the canine parainfluenza virus, canine adenovirus 2 (canine distemper virus), and canine adenovirus 1.

Responsible bacterial agents include bordetella bronchiseptica (the most common), streptococcus, pasteurella, pseudomonas, e. coli, and mycoplasma.

Although there is some debate over the effectiveness of the vaccination, it is required by many grooming, boarding, and day care facilities.

Lyme Disease

Lyme disease is caused by *Borrelia burgdorferi* and is spread by deer ticks. The prevalence varies by region. Symptoms include lameness, fever and lack of appetite.

Again, the effectiveness of the vaccine is a matter of some debate, but increasingly owners are requesting that it be administered. In part this is due to the misunderstanding that pets can transmit the disease to their owners. Humans can get Lyme disease, but only from the same ticks that infect dogs with the illness.

The Debate Over Vaccinations

Although once taken as a standard assumption that a companion animal would receive basic vaccinations followed by boosters, there is now more consideration and debate about whether or not to give vaccinations and in what combination.

It's always important to weigh the real risk of the animal contracting a specific disease, whether due to geographic location or the potential for coming into contact with other dogs.

This consideration is balanced against the probably severity of the disease in relation to the dog's age and existing state of health. The length and effectiveness of the conveyed immunity must also be considered.

Of the vaccinations discussed here, most veterinarians would likely consider rabies, distemper, and parvovirus "musts," however; the Tibetan Mastiff breed can be sensitive to vaccines and other medications, including anesthetics. Therefore, finding a vet knowledgeable with these dogs is essential.

Spaying and Neutering

Spaying and neutering procedures to sterilize companion dogs and prevent reproduction are meant to stem the tide of unwanted domestic pets, but it should also be understood that the surgeries have medical and behavioral benefits.

If a female is spayed before she goes into heat for the first time, her risk of developing mammary cancer will be greatly reduced. For males, neutering helps to prevent testicular cancer and is believed to reduce the risk of prostate problems.

For both genders, sterilization can provide a limited decrease in aggressive tendencies toward other dogs and may diminish roaming behaviors, urine marking, and inappropriate mounting.

Spaying requires a midline abdominal incision to enable removal of the uterus and both ovaries. Neutering of a male dog involves the removal of both testicles or the injection of a solution in each testicle to cause the sperm-producing cells to atrophy.

Any female Tibetan Mastiff that will not become part of a breeding program should be spayed before the age of 8 months. Males should be neutered at the point when their sexually aggressive behavior becomes a problem.

Fleas

It's unrealistic to believe that your dog won't, at some point in his life, have fleas. Particularly in the warm months, these external parasites are the bane of most dog owner's lives, but the parasites are no fun for the dog either!

Flea bites cause constant itching. If a dog scratches itself to the point of injury, open sores can develop that are subject to dangerous infection.

Fleas are very efficient at what they do. A female flea can consume 15 times her own weight in blood daily and lay up to 40 eggs. Add to those impressive abilities a very good resistance to insecticides, and it's easy to believe fleas are not only infesting our pets, but also mocking our eradication efforts in the process!

Flea prevention products must be used with care with a Tibetan Mastiff. The breed is sensitive to chemicals, so that flea control by more traditional means may be the best option.

Bathe the dog with mild shampoo especially formulated for pets. Using a flea comb (one with very narrowly spaced tines) groom the coat daily. Fleas become trapped in the tines of the comb, which is then repeatedly submersed in a glass of hot, soapy water to kill the parasites.

Vacuum floors and carpets and discard the vacuum bags at a location well away from the house. If necessary, shampoo the carpets and take up and wash all rugs. Launder the dog's bedding daily until you are sure you have the flea problem under control.

Use an insect growth inhibitor product (pyriproxyfen, methoprene, fenoxycarb) or a development inhibitor (lufenuron) to treat household surfaces rather than some form of insecticide.

Although treatments that contain chemicals like fipronil, imidacloprid, selamectin and permethrin are believed to be safe for use on pets, there have been many reports of companion dogs become quite ill or dying after their owners applied these anti-flea mixtures.

Chapter 6 – Tibetan Mastiff Health

Check the dog routinely for the presence of fleas by looking behind the ears, under the armpits, and at the base of the tail for live fleas or flea "dirt." This material, which looks like specks of tiny black gravel is actually excreted blood.

More natural strategies for flea control include:

- Dusting the dog with natural flea powders containing citronella, rosemary, wormwood, pennyroyal, and eucalyptus.

- Adding brewer's yeast and fresh garlic to the dog's morning meal.

- Sprinkling diatomaceous earth on the carpet, furniture, and pet bedding. The fleas dry up and die

Chapter 6 – Tibetan Mastiff Health

after ingesting the substance, which is the fossilized remains of single-cell algae.

If fleas are infesting your carpet and you can do so, buy the stalk from which bunches of bananas grow. These are sometimes available in open-air farmer's markets.

Put the stalk down on the floor overnight. The adult fleas will crawl inside the stalk where they become trapped. Burn the stalk and shampoo the carpet to kill any remaining eggs.

Ticks

Ticks are arachnids and are thus kin to spiders. They are also bloodsucking parasites linked to the transmission of disease including Lyme disease. The good news, however, is that a tick must be attached for 24-72 hours before it spreads disease.

Any time you've taken your Tibetan Mastiff for a stroll in a wooded or grassy area, especially during the warm months of the year, inspect the animal for ticks when you return home. While this is tricky with an animal as heavily furred as the Tibetan Mastiff, it is a necessary precaution. Pay particular attention behind and in the ears, under the arms, around the tail, and on the belly.

In removing a tick, it's important to make sure the head and mouthparts do not remain embedded in your pet's skin where they will form a painful sore. A reliable method is to coat the entire tick in petroleum jelly.

Leave the material in place for several seconds. It will clog the holes in the exoskeleton through which the tick breathes, forcing it to release its jaws. In most case when the jelly is wiped away, the tick simply comes off with it.

Clean and disinfect the area of the bite, and make sure to wash your hands with antibacterial soap. Dispose of the tick in a container of alcohol or household bleach.

Mosquito Control and Heartworms

Although a Tibetan Mastiff's thick coat offers better protection than that of many breeds, mosquitoes still pose a significant danger to your pets because they carry deadly heartworms.

All dogs should be on an ongoing program of heartworm prevention. This is one of the first topics you should discuss with your vet. Beyond that, you should also actively practice mosquito control in your yard, and never allow pools of water to stand during the warm months.

During periods of intense mosquito activity, or when there are warning about heartworms, keep your pet indoors as much as possible.

The parasite, *Dirofilaria Immitis*, is transmitted by a mosquito bite. The long, thin worms take up residence in the cardiac muscle. There, they cause bleeding and blocked blood vessels, which over time will lead to heart failure and death.

Dogs with heartworms are subject to coughing and fainting and exhibit a marked intolerance for exercise.

Internal Parasites

During your puppy's initial evaluation at the vet, you may be asked to bring in a fresh stool sample to be tested for various types of internal parasites or "worms."

These can be addressed with any one of a number of deworming agents, followed by a second course of treatment in 10 days to make sure all remaining eggs have been eliminated.

It is unlikely that a Tibetan Mastiff puppy from a reputable kennel will have worms, but any dog at any age can be afflicted with these parasites. Roundworms are often detected when the owner sees small white granules around the dog's anus.

Microscopic examination of a stool sample is needed to diagnose the presence of other types of parasites like tapeworms that can be life threatening if allowed to live in the host animal long term.

All of the following measures will help lessen the chances that your dog will contract various types of worm infestations:

- Maintain a clean and sanitary environment for the animal both inside and out.

- Clean up the dog's feces and do not allow your pet to sniff or to consume the droppings left by other dogs.

- Control fleas and ticks.

- Practice other forms of pest control to prevent infestations of lice, beetles, cockroaches, mice, and rats.

- Do not allow the dog to eat raw meat, especially poultry, or to feed on the carcasses of dead animals.

- Follow a veterinarian recommended program of heartworm prevention.

- Schedule regular stool samples for your pet.

- Do not allow your pet to roam.

Hot Spots

Pyotramatic or moist dermatitis, colloquially known as a "hot spot," is a red, inflamed, oozing, and infected area of skin that is both painful and very itchy. It is typically accompanied by hair loss.

During periods of heavy rain and in warm, humid climates Tibetan Mastiffs (and other breeds) are prone to developing hot spots, which can be treated by cleaning the area with hydrogen peroxide prior to applying cornstarch or antifungal spray powder.

Severe hot spots can develop into staph infections, so if the lesion does not clear up, seek veterinary treatment for your pet.

Entropion and Ectropion

Tibetan Mastiffs sometimes suffer from abnormalities of the eyelids, with the most common conditions being entropion and ectropion.

With entropion, the eyelid turns inward, causing the eyelashes to irritate the cornea of the eye. Ectropion is the opposite condition. One of the eyelids, usually the lower, turns outward.

The problems are believed to be genetic, and may be related to the size and shape of the dog's head or even to the presence of too much loose skin on the face.

If puppies are affected with either condition, the fact is usually obvious within the first few weeks of life. They will either squint or the eye will tear copiously, or, in the case of ectropion, the red tissue or conjunctiva that surrounds the eye will be visible.

Thankfully, both conditions are typically temporary and the dog literally grows out of it, with the eyelids normalizing, but in some cases the services of a canine ophthalmologist will be required. It is extremely important to consult with such a specialist in persistant cases of either abnormality to protect the dog's vision.

Often the lids are repositioned by means of a few "tacking" stitches, which will remain in place no more than a few days to weeks.

A second tacking procedure may be required to continue directing the growth of the lids. Artificial tears may also be placed in the eyes with an eyedropper during this period to keep the young dog more comfortable. Only in rare cases is more invasive surgical correction required.

Clearly the comfort and well being of the dog is the most important consideration, but it is worth noting that a dog that has surgically corrected entropion or ectropion can no longer be entered in dog shows. Those whose eyelids have only been tacked are still eligible for exhibition, however.

Hip and Elbow Dysplasia

Like many heavier breeds, Tibetan Mastiffs can suffer from both hip and elbow dysplasia, which is caused by a malformation of the affected ball and socket joint.

The issue can be either an overly tight fit that restricts motion, or chronic dislocations. Over time, arthritis complicates the situation even further. Severity of the dysfunction may range from a mild annoyance to severe pain.

The initial indication that dysplasia is present presents with an abnormal gait or limp that has been described as "bunny-hopping." This can be evident as early as four months of age. The cause may be genetic or the result of physical injury, overly rapid growth, or obesity. Treatment can be as simple as managing pain with medication and anti-inflammatory drugs, or can involve surgery.

Canine Inherited Demyelinative Neuropathy

Canine Inherited Demyelinative Neuropathy (CIDN) is the most rare genetic disorder identified in Tibetan Mastiffs. It is a nerve disorder that presents in otherwise normal puppies before six weeks of age. The initial sign is weakness in the hindquarters that progresses to total paralysis.

Specifically, the condition affects the nerve fibers between the spinal cord and muscles, causing the protective myelin sheath over the nerves to degenerate. There is no cure, and sufferers die by 4 months of age.

The closest human corollary illness is muscular dystrophy. Incidents of CIDN were particularly evident in one line of dogs in the early 1980s. The dogs that were tested and identified as carriers were removed from breeding programs and it is believed there are no longer any living carriers of the affected gene.

Hypertrophic Cardiomyopathy

Although a relatively rare condition, hypertrophic cardiomyopathy (HCM) does present more frequently in Tibetan Mastiffs than in other breeds. The disease causes the walls of the heart to thicken, decreasing blood flow in the body and improperly filling the chambers of the heart.

HCM often progresses into full-blown congestive heart failure.

HCM affects male dogs most often, especially those under three years of age. Generally there are no symptoms until the condition is advanced, at which time the animal will cough, have shortness of breath, and be unable to tolerate a normal level of activity. In other cases, there is no sign of illness until the dog dies of sudden heart failure.

Diagnosis will begin with an X-ray, which may show enlargement of the left chamber of the heart. A build-up of fluid in the lungs is also typical.

It is not unusual, however, for the dog to have both normal blood pressure and a normal EKG. The only real way to confirm a diagnosis of HCM is with an echocardiograph.

Although measures can be taken to make the dog more comfortable, there is no cure for HCM, and ultimately the condition is fatal.

The Cost of Veterinary Care

Over the past 25 years, there have been tremendous advances in the area of veterinary medicine. There are more available and effective treatment options than ever before, but few if any could be termed inexpensive.

That fact does not stop pet owners, however, who will spend an estimated $58.51 billion caring for their furry friends in the United States alone in 2014. It is not unusual for dog owners to sell prized possessions or to take out loans to pay for healthcare procedures for their animals.

This fact is the driving force behind the evolution of healthcare insurance for pets. Although still a relatively new product, carrying a policy on your pet can greatly defray the costs of unexpected and large vet bills.

Regular annual care for a dog is estimated to be around $277 / £162, but emergency procedures, surgery, or cancer treatments can be very costly.

Pet insurance products are sufficiently flexible that it is possible to customize policies to choose your deductible levels and copay / agreed excess levels to reach affordable premium costs.

Reimbursement protocols are slightly different with pet insurance products. Typically you pay the vet and file the claim with the company, which forwards a reimbursement check to you.

Comprehensive canine policies covering accidents, illnesses, and some hereditary conditions with optional chronic condition coverage can be purchased for $25-$35 / £14.56-£20.39 per month with up to $14,000 / £9100 a year in benefits.

Premiums at that level can equal or exceed the estimated annual average, but most pet owners agree, without hesitation, that they spend more each year at the vet than the projected average.

Chapter 6 – Tibetan Mastiff Health

Proper husbandry for any companion canine also includes preventive healthcare including, but not limited to:

- wellness checks
- heartworm prevention
- dental exams
- periodic fecal tests

Since each of these procedures carries an individual cost in addition to the routine office fee, pet insurance typically "pays for itself" rather quickly.

Chapter 7 – Showing Tibetan Mastiffs

The world of the dog fancy is not for everyone. If you think, however, that both you and your dog would enjoy the show ring and the show circuit, there are some immediate questions you should ask yourself.

For starters, did you purchase a show quality puppy? No matter how outstanding you believe your pet to be, or what a great dog he really is, if he does not sufficiently conform to the accepted show standard for the breed, there is no point to becoming involving in the dog fancy.

If you did purchase a show quality puppy, some other points to consider include:

- Is the puppy old enough to show? Six months or older?

- Is the dog registered with the appropriate kennel club sponsoring the event?

- Do you have the time to devote to learning to show your dog? And for preparing the animal to be shown?

- If not, can you afford to hire a handler to work with the dog?

- Can you afford the associated travel costs? Equipment? Entry fees? Vets bills?

Chapter 7 – Showing Tibetan Mastiffs

It is not the purpose or scope of this book to teach a Tibetan Mastiff owner to successfully show dogs. If you truly believe you are interested in dog shows, both you and your pet have a lot to learn.

You will have much better results if you begin the training process with a puppy. Older dogs are already set in their ways and even the best-behaved Tibetan Mastiff has a very definite opinion about the world and his place in it.

Given this fact, investigate the culture of the dog fancy in advance of adopting your Tibetan Mastiff puppy. Having contacts in place and already understanding the fundamentals of the special show training your dog will require may affect some of your adoption decisions.

Dog Show Basics

At a dog show individual animals in the same breed compete against one another, with a judge selecting a "Best of Breed" winner. Those dogs then compete against one another by class. For instance, all the working dogs compete in groups, with the "Group" winners then being considered for Best in Show.

Dog shows are sometimes referred to as a "conformation" shows, meaning that the judge evaluates each dog on the basis of how the animal conforms to the breed standard, which is the published criteria for an ideal representative of that particular type of dog.

There is often a feeling that in the breed specific classes what really happens is that the judge more directly compares the animals in the ring against one another rather than by their precise conformation to the standard.

However, once the animals reach the Group and Best in Show judging, conformation standards are clearly the only legitimate means for comparing a diverse group of dogs. Good handling and presentation are also essential in all classes.

The Judges

Make no mistake. Judges at dog shows are highly qualified and specifically trained in each breed they evaluate. Judges at American Kennel Club shows are required to pass written breed exams. Each applicant must:

- Have spent a minimum of 10 years as a dog owner, breeder, and exhibitor.

- Owned and exhibited several dogs of the breed to be judged.

- Bred and raised at least four litters of puppies.

- Produced at least two champions from among those four litters.

- Worked as a steward at five or more shows sanctioned by the American Kennel Club.

- Judged a minimum of six American Kennel Club matches, sweepstakes, or futurities.

The applicable written tests cover the specific breed standard as well as the American Kennel Club rules and procedures. Breed knowledge must also be proven in an oral interview.

Newly approved judges then complete five provisional assignments while being observed by an American Kennel Club field representative. Judges fully approved to work with one breed must wait a year before applying to work with a second breed.

These and additional rules governing the education and behavior of judges ensure that only highly trained professionals with an intimate knowledge of the dog fancy enter the show ring to evaluate entrants.

Some Dog Show Terminology

Like all sub-cultures, the dog fancy and dog shows have a "lingo" all their own. As you begin to read about and understand more about this world, here are some of the terms you will encounter:

- **Best of Breed** – This is the dog the judge selects as the best representative of his type at the show. Dogs may also be chosen as Best of Variety. Both awarded dogs then advance to group competition.

Chapter 7 – Showing Tibetan Mastiffs

- **Best of Opposite Sex** – This is the dog of the opposite sex selected for Best of Breed or Best of Variety. Typically these dogs advance no farther in the show.

- **Variety** - A variety is a designated division of breed based on coat, color, or size. For instance Miniature Poodle or Black Cocker Spaniels.

- **Award of Merit** – An award of merit is given at a judge's discretion for outstanding entries that do not receive Best of Breed or Best of Variety recognition.

- **Best in Show** - The Best in Show award is given to one of seven finalists and designates the dog that is the best among all entries at the show.

- **Champion** – The specific requirements for championship status vary by governing organization, but in American Kennel Club shows the dog must earn 15 point in competition with wins in AKC shows.

- **Breeder-Owner-Handler** – This means that the person who is showing the dog bred the animal, owns it, and is serving as its handler.

- **Breeder-Judge** – An individual licensed to judge dogs of their breed.

- **Professional-Handler** – An individual who handles show dogs owned by others for a fee.

Chapter 7 – Showing Tibetan Mastiffs

- **All Rounder** – A judge licensed to evaluate every breed.

- **Conformation** - The term referring to a dog's physical characteristics and structure.

- **Stack** - The term stack refers to both the pose and the act of posing the dog by the hander. It is a natural stance intended to facilitate judging of the dog according to the breed standard.

- **Gait** – A dog's gait refers to the action of the animal's movement, which should be balanced and sound, indicating correct structure and conformation.

- **Benched Show** – At a benched show the dogs must be on assigned benches when they are not in the ring being judged. This allows everyone at the show from spectators to handlers and owners to interact with the animals, ask questions, and share information.

- **Catalog** - The show catalog is a compiled listing by breed of all the dogs entered in the show. Information given includes such things as armband numbers, birthdates, sire and dam, breeders and owners.

Clearly these are not all the terms that make up the language of the dog fancy. When you attend dog shows and hear a term you don't understand, make a note to look it up later or ask. People at dog shows only love one thing more than showing their dogs – talking about them!

Join a Breed Club

After attending a dog show, if you are still interested in showing your Tibetan Mastiff, join a local or area dog club. This will help you to make friends already knowledgeable in the dog fancy, and maybe even meet other Tibetan Mastiff owners.

These are the people who will help you learn the culture of dog shows from the inside. Club membership also facilitates introductions with the contacts necessary to either learn to show your dog yourself, or to locate a proper handler.
If you have no idea where to begin finding a dog club or how to become an active member of the dog fancy and the show circuit with your Tibetan Mastiff, start with:

- The American Tibetan Mastiff Association (www.tibetanmastiff.org)

- The Tibetan Mastiff Club of America, (www.tmcamerica.org)

- The Tibetan Mastiff Club of Great Britain (www.tmcgb.net)

Chapter 8 – Tibetan Mastiff Breeders

United States

Comancheria (Alabama)
www.comancheriatms.com

Denali Legend (Alaska)
www.geocities.ws/shannygirlme

Drakyi (California)
www.tibetanmastiff.com

Araluen (Colorado)
www.araluenkennel.com

Dunebridge (Connecticut)
www.dunebridge.com

Aujudon (Georgia)
www.aujudontibetanmastiffs.com

ADynasty (Illinois)
www.adynasty-tibetan-mastiff.com

Panchen (Indiana)
www.facebook.com/panchen.tibetanmastiffs

Nyingma (Massachusetts)
www.mytibetanmastiffs.com

Chapter 8 – Tibetan Mastiff Breeders

SnowSpirits (Michigan)
www.snowspiritstibetanmastiffs.com

Majestic (Minnesota)
www.majestic-tibetan-mastiffs.com

Snow Lion (New Jersey)
www.snowliontibetanmastiffs.com/Snow_Lion_White_Tibetan_Mastiffs/Stud_Service.html

Dawa (Oregon)
dawatm.com/index2.php

Ruffini (Utah)
www.ruffini.i8.com

Himalaya (Virginia)
www.tibetan-mastiffs.net

Alaska (Washington)
www.alaskareds.net

Washani (Wisconsin)
www.washanitm.com

United Kingdom

FallenOak
www.fallenoak-tibetanmastiff.co.uk

Carramia Tibetan Mastiffs
www.tibetanmastiff.me.uk

Chapter 8 – Tibetan Mastiff Breeders

Darchen Tibetan Mastiffs
www.darchen.co.uk

Icebreaker Tibetan Mastiffs
www.icebreakertibetanmastiffs.co.uk

Bheara Tibetan Mastiffs
www.bheara.co.uk/index.html

Montasamara Tibetan Mastiffs
www.montasamara.co.uk

Smokiex Tibetan Mastiffs
www.smokiex.com

Chortens Tibetan Mastiffs
www.uktibetanmastiffs.co.uk

Afterword

Clearly the Tibetan Mastiff is not a "beginner's" dog. They are not only extremely expensive animals, but also highly specialized due to their origins in the limited confines of the high Tibetan tableland. Their role as guardians in their native environment was not just practical but also culturally significant.

Outside of Tibet, and in the hands of an inexperienced or ill-prepared owner, the dogs have often suffered greatly. Some of the earliest specimens taken to Great Britain died due to poor husbandry, including exposure to damp conditions they cannot tolerate.

It might seem common sense, for instance, to shave a dog with such a heavy coat during warm months, but that is absolutely the wrong thing to do with this species. The coat acts as insulation in both heat and cold and should always be left intact.

A Tibetan Mastiff is not an attack dog and cannot be trained to protect in that way. Although they can be quite ferocious, their primary instinct is to guard with intimidation. They are independent thinkers and feel a need to patrol and to police everything they perceive to be part of their "job."

Boredom is a recipe for trouble with a Tibetan Mastiff. If they have nothing to guard, they'll create an "assignment" in their own minds. Suddenly the pool man is an intruder, or that lawn chair leaning against the back door is an

Afterword

"enemy." The dog will go over a high fence not to run away, but to go on his appointed "rounds."

From an early age a Tibetan Mastiff must be trained to understand what is expected of him in his world. There must be a strong bond with the owner that includes real time and positive interaction. They need affection and attention and can become deeply lonely.

If the only reason you are interested in the Tibetan Mastiff is the fact that they are rare and huge, you need to rethink your motivations. There are other large dog breeds that are easier to train and are much less costly.

The primary motivating factor in adopting a living animal should always be the welfare of the dog. The real question you need to ask yourself is, "Can I provide a good home for this breed, emotionally and physically?" Be honest!

No dog surrendered to shelters or rescue groups faces an easy future, but Tibetan Mastiffs are extremely difficult to place. Most breeders will take dogs back if the adoption doesn't work out, but even that is very hard on the animal.

All dogs like constancy and routine in their lives, but the Tibetan Mastiff needs "known" elements even more than other breeds.

The Tibetan Mastiff breed is growing in popularity as a pet, but they are not dogs to be adopted lightly or on impulse. If possible you should connect with existing Tibetan Mastiff owners, meet their animals, and discuss life with the breed.

Afterword

Join a dog club or attend a dog show where Tibetan Mastiffs are being exhibited in order to make connections.

Do all of this BEFORE you start discussing available puppies and price points. Really take the time to decide if this is the breed for you. Will a Tibetan Mastiff fit in your life in a positive and healthy way – *for the dog*?

Appendix 1 - Breed Standard – United States

The following section of the book is reproduced verbatim from the breed standard for the Tibetan Mastiff and is provided here for reference purposes only. No changes have been made save those in typographical presentation.

Source:
https://www.akc.org/breeds/tibetan_mastiff/breed_standard.cfm

General Appearance

Noble and impressive: a large, but not a giant breed. An athletic and substantial dog, of solemn but kindly appearance. The Tibetan Mastiff stands well up on the pasterns, with strong, tight, cat feet, giving an alert appearance.

The body is slightly longer than tall. The hallmarks of the breed are the head and the tail. The head is broad and impressive, with substantial back skull, the eyes deep-set and almond shaped, slightly slanted, the muzzle broad and well-padded, giving a square appearance.

The typical expression of the breed is one of watchfulness. The tail and britches are well feathered and the tail is carried over the back in a single curl falling over the loin, balancing the head. The coat and heavy mane is thick, with coarse guard hair and a wooly undercoat.

The Tibetan Mastiff has been used primarily as a family and property guardian for many millennia. The Tibetan

Mastiff is aloof and watchful of strangers, and highly protective of its people and property.

Size, Proportion, Substance:

- Dogs - preferred range of 26 to 29 inches at the withers.

- Bitches - preferred range of 24 to 27 inches at the withers.

Dogs and bitches that are 18 months or older and that are less than 25 inches at the withers in the case of dogs or 23 inches at the withers in the case of bitches to be disqualified.

All dogs and bitches within the preferred range for height are to be judged equally, with no preference to be given to the taller dog.

Proportion - Slightly longer than tall (10-9), (i.e., the length to height, measured from sternum to ischium should be slightly greater than the distance from withers to ground).

Substance - The Tibetan Mastiff should have impressive substance for its size, both in bone, body and muscle.

Head: Broad, strong with heavy brow ridges. Heavy wrinkling to be severely faulted; however a single fold extending from above the eyes down to the corner of the mouth acceptable at maturity. A correct head and expression is essential to the breed.

Appendix 1 - Breed Standard – United States

Expression- Noble, intelligent, watchful and aloof. Eyes - Very expressive, medium size, any shade of brown. Rims to be black except in blue/grey and blue/grey and tan dogs, the darkest possible shade of grey.

Eyes deep-set, well apart, almond-shaped, and slightly slanting, with tightly fitting eye rims at maturity. Any other color or shape to be severely faulted since it detracts from the typical expression.

Ears - Medium size, V-shaped, pendant, set-on high, dropping forward and hanging close to head. Raised when alert, level with the top of the skull. The ear leather is thick, covered with soft short hair, and when measured, should reach the inner corner of the eye. Low-set and/or hound-like ears to be severely faulted.

Skull - Broad and large, with strongly defined occiput. Broad, flat back skull. Prominent, bony brow ridges. Stop- Moderately defined, made to appear well defined by presence of prominent brow ridges.

Muzzle - Broad, well filled and square when viewed from all sides. Proportions - Measurement from stop to end of nose to be between one-half to one-third the length of the measurement from the occiput to stop. Longer muzzle is a severe fault. Width of skull measured from ear set to opposite ear set, to be slightly greater than length of skull measured from occiput to stop (i.e., just off square).

Nose - Broad, well pigmented, with open nostrils. Black, except with blue/grey or blue/grey and tan dogs, the

Appendix 1 - Breed Standard – United States

darkest shade of grey and brown dogs, the darkest shade of brown. Any other color to be severely faulted.

Lips - Well developed, thick, with moderate flews and slightly pendulous lower lips.
Bite - Scissor bite, complete dentition, level bite acceptable.
Teeth - Canine teeth large, strong, broken teeth not to be faulted.

Disqualifications - Undershot or overshot bite.

Neck, Topline, Body:

Neck - The neck is well muscled, moderately arched, sufficient in length to be in balance with the body, and may have moderate dewlap around the throat. The neck, especially in mature dogs, is shrouded by a thick upstanding mane.

Topline - Topline level and firm between withers and croup.

Body - The chest is well developed, with reasonable spring of rib. Brisket reaching to just below elbows. Underline with pronounced (but not exaggerated) tuck-up. The back is muscular with firmly muscled loin. There is no slope or angle to the croup.

Tail - Well feathered, medium to long, not reaching below the hock, set high on line with the back. When alert or in motion, the tail is always carried curled over the back, may be carried down when dog is relaxed.

Appendix 1 - Breed Standard – United States

Faults-Double curl, incomplete curl, uncurled or straight tail. Severe faults - Tail not carried in the proper position as set forth above.

Forequarters:

Shoulders - Well laid back, muscular, strongly boned, with moderate angulation to match the rear angulation.

Legs: Straight, with substantial bone and muscle, well covered with short, coarse hair, feathering on the back, and with strong pasterns that have a slight slope.

Feet -Cat feet. Fairly large, strong, compact, may have feathering between toes. Nails may be either black and/or white, regardless of coat color. A single dewclaw may be present on the front feet.

Hindquarters: Hindquarters – Powerful, muscular, with all parts being moderately angulated. Seen from behind, the hind legs and stifle are parallel.

The hocks are strong, approximately one-third the overall length of the leg, and perpendicular. Feet - A single or double dewclaw may be present on the rear feet. Removal of rear dewclaws, if present, optional.

Coat: In general, dogs carry noticeably more coat than bitches. The quality of the coat is of greater importance than length. Double-coated, with fairly long, thick coarse guard hair, with heavy soft undercoat in cold weather which becomes rather sparse in warmer months. Hair is fine but hard, straight and stand-off; never silky, curly or wavy.

Heavy undercoat, when present, rather woolly. Neck and shoulders heavily coated, especially in dogs, giving mane-like appearance.

Tail and britches densely coated and heavily feathered. The Tibetan Mastiff is shown naturally.

Trimming is not acceptable except to provide a clean cut appearance of feet and hocks. Dogs are not to be penalized if shown with a summer coat.

Color: Black, brown, and blue/grey, all with or without tan markings ranging from a light silver to a rich mahogany; also gold, with shades ranging from a pure golden to a rich red gold. White markings on chest and feet acceptable.

Tan markings may appear at any or all of the following areas: above eyes as spots, around eyes (including spectacle markings), on each side of the muzzle, on throat, on lower part of front forelegs and extending up the inside of the forelegs, on inside of rear legs showing down the front of the stifle and broadening out to the front of the rear legs from hock to toes, on breeches, and underside of tail.

Undercoat, as well as furnishings on breeches and underside of tail, may be lighter shades of the dominant color. The undercoat on black and tan dogs also may be grey or tan.

Appendix 1 - Breed Standard – United States

Sabling, other than wolf sable and sabling in a saddle marked color pattern, is acceptable on gold dogs.

Large white markings, to be faulted. Disqualifications - All other coat colors (e.g., white, cream, wolf sable, brindle and particolors) and markings other than those specifically described.

Gait: The gait of a Tibetan Mastiff is athletic, powerful, steady and balanced, yet at the same time, light-footed and agile.

When viewed from the side, reach and drive should indicate maximum use of the dog's moderate angulation. At increased speed, the dog will tend to single-track. Back remains level and firm.

Sound and powerful movement more important than speed.

Temperament: The Tibetan Mastiff is a highly intelligent, independent, strong willed and rather reserved dog. He is aloof with strangers and highly protective of his charges and his property.

In the ring he may exhibit reserve or lack of enthusiasm, but any sign of shyness is unacceptable and must be severely faulted as inappropriate for a guardian breed.

Faults: The foregoing description is that of the ideal Tibetan Mastiff. Any deviation from the above described dog must be penalized to the extent of the deviation.

Appendix 1 - Breed Standard – United States

Disqualifications:

- Dogs under 25 inches (at 18 months or older).
- Bitches under 23 inches (at 18 months or older).
- Undershot or overshot bite. All other coat colors (e.g., white, cream, wolf sable, brindle and particolors) and markings other than those specifically described.

Approved February 10, 2012
Effective February 29, 2012

Relevant Websites

American Tibetan Mastiff Association
www.tibetanmastiff.org

Tibetan Mastiff Rescue, Inc.
www.tibetanmastiffrescueinc.org

American Kennel Club
www.akc.org/breeds/tibetan_mastiff/index.cfm

Tibetan Mastiff Info
www.tibetanmastiffinfo.com

Mastiff Club of America
www.mcoamastiff.com/MCOARESCUE.htm

The Furry Critter Network
www.furrycritter.com/resources/dogs/Tibetan_Mastiff.htm

Veterinary Pet Insurance Article on Tibetan Mastiffs
www.petinsurance.com/healthzone/pet-articles/pet-breeds/Tibetan-Mastiffs.aspx

Tibetan Mastiff Breed Guide
www.breedguide.net/dog-breed/tibetan-mastiff

The Tibetan Mastiff Club of Great Britain
www.tmcgb.net

Tibetan Mastiff – Vetstreet
www.vetstreet.com/dogs/tibetan-mastiff

Relevant Websites

Tibetan Mastiff History as a Military Working Breed
www.kesangcamp.com/index_files/page0001.htm

Principles of Canine Nutrition
www.petmd.com/dog/nutrition/evr_dg_principles_of_dog_nutrition

Dog's Social Hierarchy
www.alldogsgym.com/content/view/106/138/

Dog Training – The Basics
www.cesarsway.com/channel/dog-training/the-basics

Training Your Dog – ASPCA
www.aspca.org/pet-care/virtual-pet-behaviorist/dog-behavior/training-your-dog

Association of Professional Dog Trainers
www.apdt.com

Glossary

Abdomen – The abdomen is the surface area of a dog's body that lies between the chest and the hindquarters. This area is also referred to as the belly.

Alpha – The dominant dog in the social structure of a canine pack that acts as the leader and decision maker for the group. There may be both an alpha male and an alpha female.

Anal glands – A dog's anal glands are located on either side of the anus. They are used to mark territory and generally deposit scent simultaneously with a bowel movement. The glands may become impacted, however, and have to be expressed. Although a groomer can perform this chore, it may be necessary to seek the assistance of a veterinarian.

Arm – A dog's arm is the region of the body lying between the shoulder and the elbow. It may also be referred to as the "upper" arm.

Attack Dog – An attack dog is one that has been trained to attack on command and is kept for this purpose. Tibetan Mastiffs are not attack dogs and they cannot be successfully trained for this purpose. They are guard dogs with a strong inherited urge to patrol and protect property and people.

Back – The portion of dog's body that extending from the withers (or shoulder) to the croup (approximately the area where the back flows into the tail) is termed the "back."

Glossary

Backyard breeder – Backyard breeders are individuals engaged in the casual breeding of purebred dogs with no regard to genetic quality or consideration of the breed standard. This does not imply any wrongdoing, and generally represents someone who simply owns a purebred and for whatever reason decides to let the animal raise a litter of puppies. (Due to the rarity of the breed, there are very few backyard breeders raising Tibetan Mastiffs.)

Bitch – The appropriate term for a female dog.

Bloat – "Bloat" is the common term for gastric dilatation volvulus, a condition also referred to as twisted stomach, gastric torsion and GDV. The stomach becomes overstretched and rotated by excessive gas content. The condition can be fatal.

Blooded – A "blooded" dog is one that is said to be purebred or pedigreed.

Breed – A breed is a race or line of dogs selected and cultivated by man from a common gene pool. All breeds have consistent physical characteristics and breed "true," meaning that a male and female of a recognized breed produces puppies that are also clearly recognizable as members of the breed.

Breed standard – A breed standard is the written "picture" of the qualities necessary for an individual dog to be regarded as a perfect specimen of a given breed. These specifications include criteria for appearance, movement, and behavior. Breed standards are formulated by a parent organization, for example, the American Kennel Club or in Great Britain, The Kennel Club.

Brows – The frontal bone in a dog's skull that forms the ridge between the eyes creates a protuberance referred to as the brow.
Buttocks – The buttocks are the hips or rump of a dog.

Castrate – The surgical process of removing a male dog's testicles for purposes of sterilization to render the dog incapable of impregnating a female.

Chest – The chest is that portion of a dog's trunk or body encased by the ribs. The Tibetan Mastiff is recognized as a breed that is both broad and deep chested, a development due in part to the breed's origins in the high altitude of the Himalayas.

Coat – The hair covering a dog is referred to as the coat. Most breeds have both an outer coat and an undercoat.

Come into Season – The phrase "come into season" refers to the point at which a female dog becomes fertile for purposes of mating.

Congenital – Any quality, particularly an abnormality, present at birth is said to be congenital. In Tibetan Mastiffs the two most prevalent are hip and elbow dysplasia and hypertrophic cardiomyopathy.

Crate – A crate is a portable container used to house a dog for transport or provided to a dog in the home as a "den."

Glossary

Crate training is instrumental in housebreaking puppies because a dog will not soil his den. Crates also cut down on instances of separation anxiety.

Dam – "Dam" is the accepted term for the female parent in a breeding pair of dogs.

Dewclaw – The dewclaw is an extra claw, or in the case of dogs, extra nail on the inside of a dog's leg. It is a rudimentary fifth toe.

Euthanize – Euthanasia is the act of relieving the suffering of a terminally ill animal by inducing a humane death, typically with an overdose of anesthesia.

Ectropion – A condition common in the Tibetan Mastiff breed in which the eyelid is rolled outward from the eyeball causing irritation of the conjunctival tissue surrounding the eye.

Entropion – A condition common in the Tibetan Mastiff breed in which the eyelid is rolled inward against the eyeball often causing scratching and laceration of the cornea.

Fancier – A fancier is a person with an exceptional interest in purebred dogs and the shows where they are exhibited. The broader culture of the dog world is colloquially referred to as the dog "fancy."

Flea – Fleas are small, wingless insects that jump. They feeds on the blood of mammals and birds and are often a nuisance parasite infesting companion animals.

Glossary

Free Feeding – Free feeding is the practice of making a constant supply of food available for a dog's consumption, generally in dry form. Free feeding is not recommended with Tibetan Mastiffs.

Groom – Grooming is the act of making a dog's coat neat by brushing, combing, or trimming.

Guard Dog - A guard dog is a dog used to guard against, and watch for, unwanted or unexpected people or animals. The dog can be taught to discriminate between familiar people and actual intruders.

Harness - A harness is a cloth or leather strap that has been shaped to fit the shoulders and chest of a dog with a ring at the top for attaching a lead. Harnesses are an alternative restraint option to the traditional collar, which can cause choking. Some harnesses are special adapted for use in motor vehicles as canine seatbelts.

Haunch Bones – The haunch bones are a dog's hipbones.

Haw – The haw is the membrane inside the corner of a dog's eye known as the third eyelid.

Head - The cranium and muzzle of a dog comprise the animal's head.

Hip Dysplasia – Hip dysplasia is a condition in dogs due to a malformation of the hip joint that is either too tight or too loose. Dysplasia can be a painful condition that severely limits movement to the point that surgical intervention is

Glossary

required, or an annoyance manageable with pain medication.

Himalayas – The Himalayas are a range of mountains extending approximately 1,500 miles (2400 km) along the border between India and Tibet. The Himalayas include More than a hundred mountains that exceed 23,600 ft / 7,200 meters in elevation.

Hindquarters – The hindquarters are the back portion of a dog's body including the pelvis, thighs, hocks, and paws.

Hock – The hock is comprised of the bones on a dog's hind leg o that form the joint between the second thigh and the metatarsus. It may also be referred to as the "true heel."

Hypertrophic Cardiomyopathy – Hypertrophic Cardiomyopathy is a genetic condition found in Tibetan Mastiffs characterized by hardening of the walls of the heart. It often is not detected until the dog collapses and dies from heart failure.

Kennel – A kennel is a facility where dogs are housed for breeding or an enclosure where dogs are kept. Many commercial kennels will not accept Tibetan Mastiffs because they must be housed and fed alone and due to their large size.

Lead – A lead is any strap, cord, or chain that is used to restrain or lead a dog. Typically the lead is attached to a ring on the animal's collar or harness. An alternate term for a lead is "leash. "

Glossary

Litter – All of the puppies born at one time to a female dog comprise a "litter."

Muzzle – The muzzle is that portion of a dog's head that lies in front of the eyes. It consists of the nasal bone, nostrils, and jaws.

Neuter – Neutering is the surgical castration of a male dog or the spaying of a female dog for purposes of sterilization to render the animals incapable of producing offspring.

Pedigree – A pedigree is the written record of a dog's genealogy. For purposes of registration, the pedigree should extend back three or more generations.

Puppy – A puppy is any dog of less than 12 months of age. Tibetan Mastiffs grow rapidly in physical size, but mature slowly, so in terms of behavior, this breed retains puppy-like characteristics well into the second year of life.

Puppy Mill – A puppy mill is an establishment that exists for the purpose of breeding as many puppies for sale as possible with no consideration of potential genetic defects. Typically dogs raised in such "businesses" are kept in deplorable conditions with little to no health care or socialization. Again, due to the rarity of the Tibetan Mastiff breed, few puppy mills attempt to market these animals.

Separation Anxiety – Separation anxiety refers to the stress and nervousness suffered by a dog left alone for any period of time. Although Tibetan Mastiffs are not recognized as a breed plagued by severe separation anxiety, almost any

Glossary

breed will become nervous after about four hours, and may act out with destructive behavior as a result.

Sire – Sire is the accepted term for the male parent in a breeding pair of dogs.

Spay – Spaying is the surgical removal of a female dog's ovaries for purposes of sterilization so that she cannot conceive a litter of puppies. There is also a conveyed health benefit in that the dog will be less susceptible to various cancers associated with the reproductive organs.

Tibet - Tibet is a plateau region in Asia lying northeast of the Himalayas, in the People's Republic of China. It is the traditional homeland of the Tibetan people and of the Tibetan Mastiff. The arid regions receives little to no rainfall and is characterized by significant temperature extremes that average 3 F to 100 F (-16-37.7 C).

Tick – A tick is a bloodsucking arachnid that attaches itself to warm-blooded vertebrates to feed. Tick control is important because the parasites can transmit diseases to companion animals and humans, including, but not limited to Lyme disease. Extreme caution should be exercised in removing ticks to that the head and mouthparts are not left behind to form a painful sore.

Training – Training refers to the basic lesson in obedience essential to inculcating good and controllable behavior in a companion animal. The training fundamentals include such things as sit, stay, down, and heel. The term "obedience training" is also commonly used to refer to this process.

Glossary

Whelping – Whelping is the accepted term for the act of giving birth puppies.

Withers – The withers are the highest point of a dog's shoulders.

Wrinkle – A wrinkle is any folding and loose skin on the forehead and foreface of a dog.

Index

abdomen, 49, 129
accidents, 104
adopting, 19, 31, 83, 84, 107, 117
alpha, 35, 68, 129
American Kennel Club, 27
Bangara Mastiff, 14
Bernese Mountain Dog, 10
Bhotia, 14, 15
bone spurs, 50
bordetella bronchiseptica, 91
breeder, 17, 19, 21, 22, 23, 24, 25, 26, 29, 67, 84, 108, 130
brush, 54, 55, 60, 61
brushing, 54, 85, 133
canine adenovirus 1, 91
canine adenovirus 2 (canine distemper virus), 91
canine husbandry, 83
Canine Inherited Demyelinative Neuropathy (CIDN), 39, 102
canine parainfluenza virus, 91
canine toothpaste, 60
car, 63, 64, 65
cataracts, 84
children, 32, 72
combing, 54, 133
dematting rake, 54, 55
dog fancy, 106, 107, 109, 111, 112
dog show, 107, 112, 118
dog toothbrushes, 60
Dogue de Bordeaux, 10
Do-khyi, 36
down, 45, 49, 55, 61, 62, 68, 70, 71, 76, 77, 79, 96, 120, 122, 124, 132, 136
dry heaving, 49
e. coli, 91
ears, 20, 55, 57, 58, 95, 96, 121
Ectropion, 38, 100, 132
entropion, 100, 101
epilepsy, 84
euthanized, 84
eyes, 38, 57, 58, 101, 119, 120, 124, 131, 135
feces, 65, 74, 99
female, 35, 56, 92, 93, 129, 130, 131, 132, 135, 136
fence, 33, 73, 117
fleas, 85, 93, 94, 95, 96, 99
Genghis Khan, 1
grooming, 54, 56, 58, 61, 91

Index

guardians, 1, 2, 12, 14, 34, 73, 116
harnesses, 75, 133
heel, 79, 80, 134, 136
Himalayan Sheepdog, 15
Himalayas, 1, 12, 131, 134, 136
hip dysplasia, 84
hot spot, 99
hypertrophic cardiomyopathy, 84, 88, 102, 131
hypertrophic cardiomyopathy (HCM), 102
infectious, 91
infectious diseases, 89
internal parasites, 98
kennel cough, 28, 90
kennels, 18, 21, 23, 66, 134
Kenny Lai, 18
Komondor, 10
Kyi Apso, 15
leash, 65, 75, 77, 78, 79, 134
lethargy, 50, 90
male, 35, 56, 93, 103, 129, 130, 131, 135, 136
Marco Polo, 1, 11
Mastiff, 1, 10, 11, 13, 14, 35, 39, 41, 56, 69, 96, 112, 117, 120, 127

metal comb, 54
microchipped, 29
microchipping, 27
mites, 58
monastery, 36
mycoplasma, 91
nail clippers, 54, 61
nail clipping, 62
Neapolitan Mastiff, 10
Nepal, 15
Newfoundland, 10
nomad, 36
obedience training, 34, 136
outdoors, 15, 74
pack, 35, 68, 69, 80, 81, 129
pain, 39, 49, 63, 85, 101, 102, 134
parainfluenza, 91
parvovirus, 89, 90, 92
pasteurella, 91
pedigree, 26, 135
periodontal disease, 85
personality, 32
Pet Passport, 27
plaque, 59, 61
pseudomonas, 91
puppies, 2, 18, 19, 20, 21, 22, 28, 29, 30, 35, 43, 44, 46, 48, 65, 69, 70, 73, 81, 85, 90, 100, 102, 108, 118, 130, 132, 135, 136, 137
Puppies, 90

Index

puppy, 98
puppy mill, 28, 30, 135
raw liver, 50
rawhide chew toys, 52
rewards, 80
scabs, 59
Shakhi, 15, 16
shampoo, 57, 94, 96
shedding, 37, 55
show quality puppy, 106
sit, 36, 76, 77, 78, 79, 80, 136
skin, 50, 55, 56, 57, 58, 96, 99, 100, 137
St. Bernard, 10
stiffness, 50
stomach, 49, 50, 51, 130
streptococcus, 91
teeth, 52, 59, 60, 85, 86, 122
testicular cancer, 93
The Kennel Club, 27, 131
Tibet, 3, 4, 11, 12, 13, 15, 38, 116, 134, 136
Tibetan Hunting Dog, 15
Tibetan Mastiff, 1, 2, 3, 4, 10, 11, 12, 13, 14, 15, 17, 18, 19, 23, 24, 31, 32, 33, 35, 36, 37, 38, 39, 40, 41, 42, 43, 44, 45, 46, 47, 48, 52, 53, 54, 55, 56, 57, 58, 59, 60, 62, 63, 65, 66, 67, 68, 69, 70, 72, 73, 74, 75, 79, 81, 82, 83, 84, 86, 87, 92, 93, 94, 96, 97, 98, 107, 112, 113, 116, 117, 118, 119, 120, 124, 125, 127, 128, 131, 132, 135, 136
Ticks, 96
tracheobronchitis, 90
travel crate, 65
traveling, 12, 27, 65
Tsang-khyi, 36
Vaccination, 89
veterinarian, 27, 29, 47, 53, 61, 63, 85, 86, 99, 129
Vitamin A, 50
water, 45, 49, 53, 57, 58, 65, 94, 97
weakness, 50, 102
weight loss, 50
worms, 85, 97, 98

Conclusion

Thank you again for buying this book! I spent months writing it. As someone who has loved these dogs for years, friends told me to share my knowledge!

I hope this book helped you decide if the **Tibetan Mastiff** dog is right for your home and to how to raise it properly.

Please Help....

Finally, if you enjoyed this book, please, please, please take the time to share your thoughts and post a review on whatever site you purchased it from. It will be greatly appreciated!

The biggest criticism is always going to be making a book specific to the 'Tibetan Mastiffs' I have tried where possible to show you how this breed is unique and why it is different. But equally it does share similarities with other dogs.

www.ingramcontent.com/pod-product-compliance
Lightning Source LLC
Chambersburg PA
CBHW060835050426
42453CB00008B/698